The Aesthetics

The Aesthetics
of Chaosmos

The Middle Ages
of James Joyce

By Umberto Eco

Translated from the Italian by Ellen Esrock

Harvard University Press
Cambridge, Massachusetts
1989

Originally published as
"Le poetiche di Joyce," by Umberto Eco,
© Gruppo Editoriale Fabbri,
Bompiani, Sonzogno, Etas S.p.A.,
Milan, 1962.

Library of Congress Cataloging-in-Publication Data

Eco, Umberto.
  [Poetiche di Joyce. English]
  The aesthetics of Chaosmos : the Middle Ages of James Joyce / by
Umberto Eco ; translated from the Italian by Ellen Esrock.
      p.   cm.
  Translation of: Le poetiche di Joyce.
  Reprint. Originally published: Tulsa, Okla. : University of Tulsa,
c1982.
  Bibliography: p.
  ISBN 0-674-00635-6
  1. Joyce, James, 1882–1941—Criticism and interpretation.
2. Joyce, James, 1882–1941—Aesthetics. 3. Medievalism in
literature. I. Title.
[PR6019.09Z532713 1989]
823'.912—dc19   88-28315
                                                                              CIP

Contents

Note to the 1989 Edition

Eco's essay on Joyce originally appeared as the final chapter of the first edition (1962) of *Opera Aperta*, most of which is now translated into English as *The Open Work* (Harvard University Press, 1989); it was then removed from subsequent editions and published separately. This separation must have been dictated purely by considerations of size, since the argument of this essay is integrally connected to the themes of *Opera Aperta*, for which Joyce's work is a constant point of reference. For Eco, Joyce is the exemplary modern, or modernist, writer. His work is the most powerful, radical, and influential embodiment of tendencies that dominate the literature and art of our time—tendencies formulated by Eco in the concept of the "open" work. *Finnegans Wake* in particular is for Eco the "open" work *par excellence*.

The Aesthetics of Chaosmos is thus a contribution to a discussion which has remained topical in a great deal of modern literary theory— a relatively early contribution that predates the explosion of literary theory in the mid-sixties, and anticipates much subsequent work. It is distinguished by a number of features that reflect Eco's particular concerns at the time he wrote it, though these concerns have also in various ways remained part of his thinking. The conception of works of art as "epistemological metaphors," which plays a major role in *Opera Aperta*, is applied with special force to Joyce, in whose evolution as a writer Eco finds an embodiment of what he considers the major development in the history of Western thought: the transition from models of rational order, expressed most fully in the *summae* of medieval Scholasticism, to the sense of chaos and crisis that dominates the modern experience of the world. Along with, and even more than, other modern "open" works, *Ulysses* and *Finnegans Wake* give form to this experience of the world, and thereby constitute in their own way a kind of knowledge, a bringing to consciousness of the nature of the modern condition. Such knowledge, Eco argues in *Opera Aperta*, is also a basis for political action; consciousness of the modern condition enables one to act upon the world to change it for the better.

There is, too, an engagingly personal aspect to Eco's discussion of

Joyce. Not only does Joyce's evolution, from Catholic, Thomist interests to a disordered vision of life, mirror Eco's; the coexistence of models of order and disorder that Eco finds in *Ulysses* has also characterized most of his own work, including *The Name of the Rose*, which so strikingly juxtaposes the harmonious, rational medieval intellectual system with the worldview expressed by William of Baskerville: a distinctively modern sense of chaos and crisis.

David Robey

Translator's Foreword

The Aesthetics of Chaosmos is a translation of Umberto Eco's Italian text Le Poetiche di Joyce (Milano: Bompiani, 1966), first published as a part of Opera Aperta (Milano: Bompiani, 1962). For the present edition, Eco has introduced one new section, "The Medieval Model," which incorporates parts of a lecture given in 1969 at Tulsa University, and he has substantially expanded one existing section, "The Poetics of the Pun." Also, as explained in the author's note, certain scholarly references have been eliminated.

The translation of Eco's work proved challenging. In addition to the expected task of recasting stylistic forms, the project required careful balancing. On the one hand, we wished to maintain the original 1960's perspective of the text. We sought, therefore, to avoid terminology that was indigenous to more contemporary models of linguistic analysis (as developed, for example, by Eco in A Theory of Semantics [Bloomington: Indiana Univ. Press, 1976]). On the other hand, the Italian text was written with an impulse towards the future. Eco's analyses foreshadowed issues that would be more fully developed within the framework of contemporary semiotics. We attempted, then, to recapture its trajectory, as well as its point of origin.

I am greatly indebted to Alice Oxman for a preliminary, partial translation of Le Poetiche di Joyce, portions of which have been incorporated into the present text. And I am grateful, of course, to Umberto Eco, for his patience in undertaking this excursion into his Joycean past. In the spirit of translator-editors, I accept responsibility for all errors.

Ellen J. Esrock
New York University, 1979

Author's Note

In publishing my Joycean adventure after twenty years I have not succumbed to the temptation to make substantial changes, even though the long work with Ellen Esrock in making the text more comprehensible has led to many cuts, especially in those parts which functioned at the time to give various items of scholarly information to Italian readers. Joyce was *also* an Italian author, and some of his highest praise came in the very beginning from the Italian literary milieu (Svevo, Benco, Montale. . .). But in 1962 *Ulysses* had been fully translated into Italian for only two years, not to mention the incomplete and tentative translations of *Finnegans Wake*. Thus my text was overloaded with explanations and bibliographical references unnecessary for the current American reader.

I have therefore retained only the parts focusing on the central theme of my research: the permanence of a medieval model, not only in the early writings but also in the later work of James Joyce.

In order to understand my curiosity, some biographical information may be helpful: I began my scholarly career studying medieval aesthetics (*Il Problema Estetico in San Tommaso* [Torino: Edizioni di "Filosofia," 1956]; "Sviluppo dell'estetica Medievale," in *Momenti e Problemi di Storia dell'estetica* [Milano: Marzorati, 1959], both works amalgamated in *Il Problema Estetico in Tommaso d'Aquino* [Milano: Bompiani, 1970]). Immediately after (but following the same interests and curiosity about the problem of structuring vs. destructuring in communication), I studied the language of contemporary avant-gardes. The study of Joyce was first published as part of my book *Opera Aperta* (Milano: Bompiani, 1962) the first chapter of which the reader can find as the first essay of my recent *The Role of the Reader* (Bloomington: Indiana Univ. Press, 1979).

To me Joyce was the node where the Middle Ages and the avant-garde meet, and the present book is the story and the historical-theoretical foundation of such a paradoxical meeting.

I have therefore chosen to keep the original perspective of my text, even though much important Joycean research has appeared since 1962. Thus I have not taken into account the challenging contributions of Thomas Staley, Bernard Benstock, Fritz Senn, Robert Scholes, David Haymann, Lulli Paci, Anthony Burgess and others, or, to speak of research more directly connected with my topic, Jacques Aubert and Jan Schoonbroodt. References to the scholarship that inspired my research prior to 1962 are listed at the end of the book, while other works, primarily concerning the Middle Ages, Renaissance philosophy, and modern science are found in the footnotes. I have expanded a paragraph on the medieval model and an analysis of puns in *Finnegans Wake* (the subject of a 1971 essay "Semantics of Metaphor," now published in *The Role of the Reader*).

I have agreed to awaken-again and make my book riverrunning in a vicus of recirculation only because of the missionary fervor of my friends at the James Joyce Foundation and *James Joyce Quarterly*, to whom we owe the fact that Martello Tower is still and again living. My debt to them should be recorded in Finneganian. That, in fact, has been done, but only in secret files lost or hidden in the meandertale connecting the "hauts lieux" of Trieste, Dublin, Paris, Zurich and Tulsa.

Umberto Eco
Milano, 1981

I. The Early Joyce

"Steeled in the school of the old Aquinas."
—James Joyce, "The Holy Office"

The term "poetics" has acquired many meanings during the centuries. Aristotle's *Poetics* is an answer to both the questions "What is Art?" and "How does one make a work of art?" The modern philosophical tradition has preferred to define the theoretical answer to the first question as "aesthetics" and to utilize "poetics" in order to describe the program of a single artist or a particular artistic school. In this context, "poetics" addresses the question "How does one make a work of art according to a personal program and an idiosyncratic world view?" The more recent definition by the Prague Linguistic School considers "poetics" as the study of "the *differentia specifica* of verbal behavior."[1] In other words, "poetics" is the study of the structural mechanism of a given text which possesses a self-focusing quality and a capacity for releasing effects of ambiguity and polysemy.

Joyce plays with all these notions of poetics throughout his works; he interweaves questions as to the concept of art, the nature of his personal artistic program, and the structural mechanisms of the texts themselves. In this respect all of Joyce's works might be understood as a continuous discussion of their own artistic procedures.

A Portrait is the story of a young artist who wants to write *A Portrait*; *Ulysses*, a little less explicit, is a book which is a model of itself; *Finnegans Wake* is, above all, a complete treatise on its own nature, a continuous definition of "the Book" as the *Ersatz* of the universe. The reader, therefore, is continually tempted to isolate the poetics proposed by Joyce in order to define, in Joycean terms, the solutions that Joyce has adopted.

Although one can discuss the poetics of Horace, Boileau, or Valéry without referring to their creative works, Joyce's poetics cannot be separated from Joyce's texts. The poetics themselves form an intimate part of the artistic creation and are clarified in the various phases of the development of his opus. The entire Joycean project might thus be seen as the development of a poetics, or rather, as the dialectical movement of various opposite and complementary poetics – the history of contemporary poetics in a game of oppositions and continuous implications.

Among the numerous cultural influences upon the young Joyce, we note three major lines which appear in all his works. On one count, we find the influence of Aquinas, thrown into crisis but not completely destroyed by the reading of Bruno and, on another, the influence of Ibsen, with a call for closer ties between art and life. Finally, we note the influence of the symbolist poets, with the aesthetic ideal of a life devoted to art and of art as a substitute for life, and with their stimulus to resolve the great problems of the spirit in the laboratory of language.[2] These contrasting influences from different centuries were assimilated within a framework that grew increasingly concerned with the problems of contemporary culture, from the psychology of the unconscious to the physics of relativity. The staggering quantity of Joyce's reading and the diversity of his interests opened the way to his discovery of new dimensions of the universe.

Approached in this way, our research needs a guiding thread, a line of investigation, an operative hypothesis. We take, therefore, the opposition between a classical conception of form and the need for a more pliable and "open" structure of the work and of the world. This can be identified as a dialectic of order and adventure, a contrast between the world of the medieval *summae* and that of contemporary science and philosophy.

Joyce himself authorizes us to use this dialectical key. The Joycean detachment from the familiar clarity of the schoolmen and his choice of a more modern and uneasy problematic is actually based on the Brunian revelation of a dialectic of contraries, on the acceptance of the *coincidentia oppositorum* of Cusano. Art and life, symbolism and realism, classical world and contemporary world, aesthetic life and daily life, Stephen Dedalus and Leopold Bloom, Shem and Shaun, order and possibility are the continuous terms of a tension that has its roots in this theoretical discovery. In Joyce's works the very crisis of late scholasticism is accelerated and therein a new cosmos is born.

But this dialectic is not perfectly articulated; it does not have the balance of those ideal triadic dances upon which more optimistic philosophies build legends. While Joyce's mind brings this elegant curve of oppositions and mediations to its limits, his unconscious agitates like the unexpressed memory of an ancestral trauma. Joyce departs from the *summa* to arrive at *Finnegans Wake*, from the ordered cosmos of scholasticism to the verbal image of an expanding universe. But his medieval heritage, from which his movements arise, will never be abandoned. Underneath the game of oppositions and resolutions in which the various cultural influences collide, on the deepest level, is the radical opposition between the medieval man, nostalgic for an ordered world of clear signs and the modern man, seeking a new habitat but unable to find the elusive rules and thus burning continually in the nostalgia of a lost infancy.

We would like to demonstrate that the definitive choice is not made and that the Joycean dialectic, more than a mediation, offers us the development of a continuous polarity between Chaos and Cosmos, between disorder and order, liberty and rules, between the nostalgia of Middle Ages and the attempts to envisage a new order. Our analysis of the poetics of James Joyce will be the analysis of a moment of transition in contemporary culture.

The Catholicism of Joyce

> I will tell you what I will do and what I will not do. I will not serve that in which I no longer believe whether it call itself my home, my fatherland or my church: and I will try to express myself in some mode of life or art as freely as I can and as wholly as I can, using for my defence the only arms I allow myself to use—silence, exile, and cunning (P 247).

With Stephen's confession to Cranly, the young Joyce proposes his own program of exile. The assumptions of Irish tradition and Jesuitical education lose their value as rules. Thus Joyce abandons the faith but not religious obsession. The presence of an orthodox past re-emerges constantly in all of his work under the form of a personal mythology and with a blasphemous fury that reveals its affective permanence. Critics have spoken a great deal of Joyce's "Catholicism." The term appropriately reflects a mentality which rejects dogmatic substance and moral rules yet conserves the exterior forms of a rational edifice and retains its instinctive fascination for rites and liturgical figurations. Evidently, we are dealing with a fascination à *rebours*; speaking about Catholicism in connection with Joyce is a bit like speaking about filial love in connection with Oedipus and Jocasta. When Henry Miller insults Joyce, calling him the descendant of a medieval erudite with "priest's blood" and speaking of his hermit's morality with the onanistic mechanism that such a life comports, he identifies, with paradoxical treachery, a distinctive feature of Joyce.

Similarly, when Valery Larbaud remarks that *A Portrait* is closer to Jesuitical casuistry than to French naturalism, he says nothing that the average reader has not already sensed. But *A Portrait* reflects something more. The narration which is tuned to liturgical time, the taste for sacred oratory and moral introspection convey not only the mimetic instincts of the narrator but also an all-pervasive psychological mood. The style, imitating that of a rejected position, does not succeed as an indictment of Catholicism. It was not by chance that Thomas Merton converted to Catholicism upon reading *A Portrait*, thereby taking a road opposite that of Stephen's. This was possible not because the ways of the Lord are infinite but because the ways of Joycean sensibility are strange and contradictory, with the Catholic thread surviving in a vague, abnormal manner.

Buck Mulligan opens *Ulysses* with his *"Introibo ad altare Dei,"* and the Black Mass is placed at the center of the work. The erotic ecstasy of Bloom and his lewd and platonic seduction of Gerty McDowell are in counterpoint with the moments of the Eucharistic ceremony performed in the church near the beach of Reverend Hughes. The macaronic Latin that appears at the end of *Stephen Hero*, which returns in *A Portrait* and appears here and there in *Ulysses*, reflects not only the speech patterns of the medieval *Vagantes* but also the patterns of their conceptual thought. Like those who abandon a discipline but not its cultural baggage, with Joyce there remains the sense of a curse celebrated according to a liturgical ritual. "Come up you, fearful jesuit," Mulligan shouts to Stephen and later clarifies, "Because you have the cursed jesuit strain in you, only it's injected the wrong way...." And in *A Portrait*, Cranly observes the curious fact that Stephen's mind is saturated with the religion that he supposedly rejects.

Similarly, references to the liturgy of the Mass appear in the most unexpected ways at the center of the puns which are woven throughout *Finnegans Wake*:

> (enterellbo add all taller Danis) (336.02).... Per omnibus secular seekalarum (81.08).... meac Coolp, (344.31)...meas minimas culpads! (483.35)....
> Crystal elation! Kyrielle elation! (528.09).... Sussumcordials (453.26)....
> —Grassy ass ago (252.13).... Eat a missal lest (456.18).... Bennydick hotfoots onimpudent stayers! (469.23)....

Here one can discern the pure taste for assonance and parody. In light of this ambivalent relationship with Catholicism, the two symbolic superstructures imposed upon *Ulysses* and *Finnegans Wake* appear clearer. The triangle of Stephen-Bloom-Molly becomes the image of the Trinity; H.C. Earwicker acquires the symbolic role of the scapegoat who assumes within himself the whole of humanity ("Here Comes Everybody"), fallen and saved by a resurrection. Stripped of any precise theological nature, involved in all myths and religions, the symbolic figure of HCE assumes coherence by respect of an ambiguous relationship to a Christ who is deformed by historical awareness and identified with the very process of history (see Robinson, 1959). In the heart of this same evolving cycle of human history, the author feels as victim and logos, *"in honour bound to the cross of your own cruelifiction."*

But the displays of Joycean Catholicism develop along more than one line. If we find, on one side, this almost unconscious, obsessive ostentation, somewhat *mal tournée*, then on the other we detect a mental attitude that is valuable at the level of operative efficacy. On the one hand, a mythical obsession, on the other, a way of organizing ideas. Here, the deposit of symbols and figures is filtered and brought to play within the framework of another faith; there, a mental habit is placed in the service of a heterodox *Summulae*. This is the second moment of Joycean Catholicism – the moment of medieval scholasticism.

Joyce attributes to Stephen "a genuine predisposition in favour of all but the 'premises of scholasticism'" (*SH* 77). According to Harry Levin, the tendency for abstraction reminds us continuously that Joyce reaches aesthetics through theology. Joyce loses his faith but remains faithful to the orthodox system. Even in his mature works, Joyce often seems to have remained a realist in the most medieval sense of the word (Levin, 1941, p. 25).

This mental structure is not exclusively a characteristic of the young Joyce who is still close to the Jesuitical influence, for the syllogistic style of reasoning survives even in *Ulysses*, if only as the distinctive mark of a pattern of thinking. As an example, consider the monologue in the third chapter or the discussion in the library. Also in *A Portrait*, though Stephen is joking by speaking in macaronic Latin, it is with maximum seriousness that he asks these kinds of questions: is baptism by mineral water valid? does the theft of a sterling and the acquisition of a fortune from it require one to restore the sterling or the entire fortune? And with greater problematic acuteness, he asks the following: if a man hacking randomly at a block of wood makes the image of a cow, is that image a work of art? These questions are of the same family as those posed by the scholastic doctors debating the *questiones quodlibetales* (one of these, by Aquinas, asks in what way the human will is most strongly determined—by wine, women, or love of God). And of a more direct scholastic origin, less influenced by counter-reformist casuistry than the preceding, is the question that Stephen asks himself: is the portrait of Mona Lisa good by the fact that I desire to see it?

It is thus necessary to ask how much of the scholasticism of the young Joyce is substantial and how much is only superficial—a mischievous taste for contamination or an attempt to smuggle revolutionary ideas under the cape of Doctor Angelicus (the technique that Stephen frequently utilizes with the college professors).

Stephen confesses to having read "only a garner of slender sentences from Aristotle's poetics and psychology and a *Synopsis Philosophiae Scholasticae ad mentem divi Thomae.*" The question that must be asked is whether or not Stephen is lying. It is of little help to discuss Joyce's reading material while he was in Paris. There is the confession to Valery Larbaud that "il passait plusieures heures chaque soir à la bibliothèque St. Geneviève lisant Aristote et St. Thomas d'Aquin." But we know the Joycean ability in mystifying his friends. His "Paris Notebook" shows that he studied the Aristotelian definitions of pity and terror, rhythm, and imitation of nature by art. This would suggest that Joyce had probably read excerpts from the *Poetics*. Where St. Thomas is concerned, the quotations in the "Pola Notebook" ("Bonum est in quo tendit appetitum [*sic*]" and "Pulcera [*sic*] sunt quae visa placent") are both misquoted, and the definition of the three conditions of Beauty in *A Portrait* is linguistically correct but abridged. From this we infer that Joyce had probably never read directly from the texts of Aquinas.[3]

The Medieval Model

What is meant by the affirmation that Joyce remained medievally minded from youth through maturity? In reading all of Joyce it is possible to single out thousands of situations in which he uses terms drawn from the medieval tradition, arguments accorded to a technique from medieval literature and philosophy. At this point, it may be helpful to construct an abstract model of the medieval way of thinking in order to demonstrate how Joyce adapts it point by point.

While the medieval thought process is certainly more complex than the proposed outline, so too is Joyce. The point of this exercise is to summarily indicate the presence of medieval patterns in the mental economy of our author.

The medieval thinker cannot conceive, explain, or manage the world without inserting it into the framework of an Order, an Order whereby, quoting Edgard de Bruyne, "les êtres s'emboitent les uns dans les autres." The young Stephen at Clongowes Wood College conceives of himself as a member of a cosmic whole—"Stephen Dedalus—Class of Elements—Clongowes Wood College—Sallins—County of Kildare—Ireland—Europe—The World—The Universe." *Ulysses* demonstrates this same concept of order by the choice of a Homeric framework and *Finnegans Wake* by the circular schema, borrowed from Vico's cyclical vision of history.

The medieval thinker knows that art is the human way to reproduce, in an artifact, the universal rules of cosmic order. In this sense art reflects the artist's impersonality rather than his personality. Art is an *analogon* of the world. Even if Joyce had discovered the notion of impersonality in more modern authors such as Flaubert, it goes without saying that his enthusiasm for this theory had medieval sources.

This framework of Order provides an unlimited chain of relations between creatures and events. Quoting Alanus ab Insulis:

> Omnis mundi creatura
> quasi liber et pictura
> nobis est in speculum.
>
> Nostrae vitae, nostrae mortis
> nostri status, nostrae sortis
> fidele signaculum.

It is the mechanism which permits epiphanies, where a thing becomes the living symbol of something else, and creates a continuous web of references. Any person or event is a cypher which refers to another part of the book. This generates the grid of allusions in *Ulysses* and the system of puns in *Finnegans Wake*. Every word embodies every other because language is a self-reflecting world. Language is the dream of history telling itself to itself. Language is a book readable by an ideal reader affected by an ideal insomnia. If you take away the transcendent God from the symbolic world of the Middle Ages, you have the world of Joyce. This operation, however, is performed by the most medieval thinkers of the Renaissance—Giordano

Bruno and Nicola da Cusa, both masters to Joyce. The world is no longer a pyramid composed of continual transcendent displacements but a self-containing circle or spiral.

For the medieval thinker, the objects and events which the universe comprises are numerous. A key, therefore, must be found to help the scholar discover and catalogue them. The first approach to the reality of the universe was of an encyclopedic type. It was the first in the sense that the great popular encyclopedias, *De Imagine Mundi*, *Specula Mundi*, *The Herbary* or *The Bestiary*, historically preceded the epoch of the great theological arrangements. It was also the first in the sense that it was the most immediate, the most familiar and remains as a mental plan in even the most elaborate philosophical treatments. The encyclopedic approach uses the techniques of the Inventory, the List, the Catalogue or, in classical rhetorical terms, the *Enumeratio*. In order to describe a place or a fact, the early poets of the Latin Middle Ages first provide a list of detailed aspects. This extract from Sidonius Apollinaris is a representative example from a potential list that would compose several volumes:

> Est locus Oceani, longiquis proximus
> Indis, axe sub Eoo, Nabateum tensus in Eurum;
> ver ibi continuum est, interpellata nec
> ullis frigoribus pallescit humus, sed
> flore perenni picta peregrino ignorant
> arva rigores; halant rura rosis,
> indiscriptosque per argos fragrat odor;
> violam, cytisum, serpylla, ligustrum,
> lilia, narcissos, casiam, colocasiax,
> caltas, costum, malobathrum, myrrhas,
> opobalsama, tura parturiunt campi; nec
> non pulsante senecta hinc redivia petit
> vicinus cinnama Phoenix (*Carmina* 2).

Here is another passage by the same author which describes, like a property map, the city of Narbona with its particular urban qualities:

> Salve Narbo, potens salubritate,
> urbe et rure simul bonus videri,
> muris, civibus, ambitu, tabernis,
> portis, porticibus, foro theatro,
> delubris, capitoliis, monetis,
> thermis, arcubus, horreis, macellis,
> pratis, fontibus, insulis, salinis,
> stagnis, flumen, merce, ponte, ponto;

unus qui venerere jure divos
Lenaem, Cererem, Palem, Minervam,
spicis, palmite, pascuis, trapetis (*Carmina* 23).

These authors compile catalogues of objects and treasures from cathedrals and kings' palaces where the seemingly casual accumulation of relics and art objects follows without clear distinctions between the beautiful work and the teratological curiosity. They obey, instead, a logic of the inventory. For example, the Treasury of the Cathedral of St. Guy in Prague (the treasury of the Cathedral of Charles IV of Bohemia) listed, among other innumerable objects, the skulls of St. Adalbert and St. Venceslas, the sword of St. Stephen, Jesus' crown of thorns, pieces of Jesus' cross, the tablecloth of the Last Supper, a tooth of St. Marguerite, a piece of the shinbone of St. Vitalis, a rib of St. Sophia, the chin of St. Eoban, the shoulderblades of St. Affia, a whale rib, the horn of an elephant, the ashplant of Moses, and the clothes of the Virgin. Included within the Treasury of the Duc du Berry were a stuffed elephant, a hydra, a basilisk, an egg within an egg found by an abbot, manna from the wilderness, the horn of a unicorn, the wedding ring of St. Joseph, and a coconut. Similarly, the Treasury of the Sacred Roman Empire in Vienna noted an imperial crown, a regal globe, the word of St. Maurice, the sphere and the nail of a saint of the Holy Cross, and a fragment of Jesus' cradle. Last but not least, the Treasury of Köln Cathedral seemingly held the skull of St. John the Baptist at twelve years of age [*sic*].

These lists curiously resemble the list of the paraphernalia of the various saints in the mystical procession which appears in the "Cyclops" chapter of *Ulysses*. Moreover, an inventory of this type, though less "liturgical," is found in the penultimate chapter of *Ulysses* ("Ithaca") when Bloom lists the objects contained in his drawer.

The technique of the inventory is also typical of primitive thought, as explained by Claude Lévi-Strauss in *La Pensée Sauvage*. The "Savage Mind" arranges the world according to a taxonomy that builds coherent wholes through the technique of *bricolage*, reconstructing a form by utilizing the parts of no longer existing forms. This procedure is typical of a medieval civilization which must reconstruct a world on the ruins of a pagan and Roman one, without yet having a precise vision of the new culture. In listing the artifacts of a past civilization, the medieval mind examines them to see if a different answer might be born from a new combination of pieces. As we will later see, this is exactly the project that Joyce proposes in destroying the form of the world given to him from traditional culture. With a medieval disposition, he examines the immense repertory of the universe reduced to language, in order to catch glimpses of new and infinite possibilities of combination.

The technique of the list returns in other areas of human history. We find it in the early Renaissance with Rabelais, and there too it was an attempt to produce a different arrangement of reality by rejecting the order imposed from academic, archaic, and scholastic culture. We discover it in Giordano Bruno (it was not by chance that Bruno was so admired by Joyce). Finally, we find it in contemporary art and in the various techniques of assemblage, collage, pop clippings, and pastings from products of a previous culture. But once again, for Joyce the first inspiration was of medieval origin. His initial model was the Litany of the Blessed Virgin and the monotonous and repetitive cyclic succession of the Rosary. We must remember that the technique of the inventory does not appear only in the narrative pages but occurs even in the technique of cultural phagocytosis that Joyce used to acquire fresh information on ancient and modern culture. It is enough to read a book like *The Books at the Wake* by Atherton to realize that Joycean culture is an immense list of texts drawn from all libraries. The young Joyce confessed to have approached St. Thomas and Aristotle across "a garner of slender sentences" (not a system but a *garner*). Even the notes and questions in his notebooks appear in lists.

Once the material which the world comprises is controlled through the preliminary inventory, the medieval thinker tries to explain the form of the universe. But he would never venture out alone in this undertaking. He must always be guaranteed the pledge of an *Auctoritas*. Although the medieval mind does not fear innovation, it conceals changes under the form of commentaries which were appended to the thoughts of a previous Great Thinker. Joyce, at least in his early works, does nothing other than smuggle in an original aesthetics as a commentary on the ideas of Aquinas. "As Aquinas says" is the formula with which the young Stephen virtually introduces every personal heresy (his Jesuit masters trembled in the face of heresy, but trembled even more at the thought of contradicting Aquinas and thereby lost themselves in dialectical subtlety in order the draw the opposite results from the same quotations). Thus Joyce, their worthy student, dragged them into his own game, which was in the beginning their game but was now turned upside down and its algebraic sign reversed. From the medieval habit of quoting in order to demonstrate, Joyce acquired the taste for quotation at any cost, even if camouflaged quotation. *Finnegans Wake*, even more than *Ulysses*, can be seen in its entirety as an immense catalogue of authoritative quotations, a *Walpurgisnacht* of philosophy à *rebours*.

It is only at this point that the medieval thinker can permit himself to betray his own masters and to confess it, at least to himself. A beautiful phrase which reflects this way of thinking is from Bernard of Chartres (then revived by others, even Newton and Gassendi) and can only be quoted through the words of Jean of Salisbury:

> dicebat Bernardus Carnotensis nos esse quasi nanos gigantium humeris insidentes ut possimus plura eis et remotiora videre, non utique proprii visus acumine aut eminentia corporis, sed quia in altum subvehimur et extollimur magnitudine gigantes.

This means that the contemporary thinker, small and incapable in respect to the giants of the past, nonetheless has the chance to hoist himself upon their shoulders and see, if only slightly, further ahead. Joyce implicitly and unconsciously adopts this quotation when he states that his is the use of an "applied Aquinas" (*SH* 77) and affirms that he has "only pushed to its logical conclusion the definitions Aquinas has given of the beautiful" (*SH* 95). This is how the young Stephen and Joyce generally reproduce the fundamental structures of a medieval way of thinking in their *modus operandi*. The following pages will explore the extent to which this heredity (the forms of thought before contents) remains alive in the work of Joyce and serves as a model through which we can understand the poetics of the author. We will attempt to follow the process of the young artist who conserves and repudiates the mental forms that preside over the ordered cosmos proposed by the medieval Christian tradition and who, still thinking as a medieval, dissolves the ordered Cosmos into the polyvalent form of the Chaosmos.

The Young Attempts

At the beginning of the century Joyce was about eighteen years old. The scholastic culture which he absorbed during high school was already facing a crisis. Joyce's contact with Giordano Bruno in these years provided him with what in fact Brunian philosophy provided for modern thought, a bridge from medievalism to the new natural-ism. During this time, Joyce was cultivating the threefold refusal that would isolate him in exile until the end. He had settled his accounts with heresy, "He said Bruno was a terrible heretic. I said he was ter-ribly burned" (*P* 249).

Having shaken off the weight of orthodoxy, Joyce was open to new suggestions which came to him from the Irish literary polemics, from the great problems stirring world literature. On the one side he was influenced by the symbolists, the poets of the Celtic Renaissance, by Pater and Wilde; on the other side, by the realism of Flaubert (as well as Flaubert's love for *le mot juste*, the dedication to an aesthetic ideal).

Four fundamental texts mark those years—the conference *Drama and Life* held in 1900, the essay "Ibsen's New Drama" published the same year in *Fortnightly Review*, the pamphlet *The Day of the Rabble-ment* published in 1901, and finally, in 1902, the essay "James Clarence Mangan." Condensed in these four writings are all the con-tradictions that raged within the young artist.

In the first two essays, Joyce argues for close connections between theater and life. The theater must represent real life "as we see it before our eyes, men and women as we meet them in the real world, not as we apprehend them in the world of faery" (*CW* 45). This representation is not mere imitation, since the theater must manifest the great rules that govern human events through the action of per-formance. In this way, art proposes truth as the primary end. Not a didactic truth (for Joyce claims an absolute moral neutrality for the artistic representation) but pure and simple truth, reality. And beauty? The search for beauty itself has something that is spiritually anemic and brutally animal. Beauty does not go beyond the surface and appears, therefore, as a morbid result of art. Great art tends only towards the pursuit of truth. Against the symbolists' idea that "tout est bu, tout est mangé! Plus rien à dire!" (Verlaine), Joyce stresses that

> Many feel like the Frenchman that they have been born too late in a world too old.... Still I think out of the dreary sameness of existence, a measure of dramatic life may be drawn. Even the most commonplace, the deadest among the living, may play a part in a great drama (*CW* 44-45).

This apparent commitment to daily life makes even more discor-dant the position upheld in the *Day of the Rabblement*, a work which vibrates with disdain for compromise with the masses and projects an ascetic type of aspiration for the withdrawal and the absolute isolation of the artist. "No man, said the Nolan, can be a lover of the true or the good unless he abhors the multitude" (*CW* 69). This withdrawal might be understood as a reserve on the level of practical contact, a refusal for commercial compromise rather than an aesthetic position were it not for the essay on Mangan.

Mangan was not a realist nor did he search for poetic truth in the representation of historical truth. He constitutes, instead, an example of the excited imagination on the border of prophecy, nourished by the exaltation of the senses, by drugs, and by an unruly and eccentric life. His poetry belongs in a romantic-symbolist line; his spiritual brothers are Nerval and Baudelaire. It is this aspect that interested Joyce. In the conference on Mangan held in 1907 at Trieste, Joyce dwelt at length on this poetry:

> It is a wild world, a world of night in the orient. The mental activity that comes from opium has scattered this world of magnificent and terrible images, and all the orient that the poet recreated in his flaming dream, which is the paradise of the opium-eater, pulsates in these pages in Apocalyptic phrases and similes and landscapes (*CW* 183).

These contradictions might seem to be the fruit of a pure, youthful intemperance, but in Joyce they appear as the germs of vast contradictions and opposing aspirations which are perpetuated through all his works. It is Joyce himself who offered the key in a conference in 1907, with a phrase referring to Mangan but which perfectly fits the "Joyce case":

> There are certain poets who, in addition to the virtue of revealing to us some phase of the human conscience unknown until their time, also have the more doubtful virtue of summing up in themselves the thousand contrasting tendencies of their era, of being, so to speak, the storage batteries of new forces (*CW* 175).

While Joyce provides an exact description of our daily humanity (in *Dubliners* as well as *Ulysses*), at the same time he discovers in Mangan an example of the revelatory function of poetry. Once again, the artist can succeed in possessing and communicating the truth, but only through beauty. Thus the situation is reversed. When Joyce speaks of beauty as the splendor of truth in the essay on Mangan, he no longer thinks of a truth that—*qua* truth—becomes beauty, but of a gratuitous beauty, born from the provocative strength of the imagination which, in fact, becomes the only possible truth.

Even when Joyce uses expressions analogous to those in the discourse on drama, he speaks unequivocally in the tone of the Mangan essay. The language is that of *fin de siècle* decadentism. Traces of occultism also shine through the discourses and reflect what Joyce had assimilated in the Dublin circle of AE, George Russell.[4] Without a doubt, Ibsen had left the post to the symbolist poets and mystics.

How could these divergent tendencies be fused in the thought of the early Joyce? At least we know how they merge in the thought of Stephen Dedalus and in what way Joyce sought to synthesize his own former attitudes when he was writing *Stephen Hero* between 1904 and 1906. The lecture "Art and Life" that Stephen reads in college before the Literary and Historical Society reunites "Drama and Life" and "J.C. Mangan." If the title recalls more the lecture on Ibsen, the subjects used – often the very expressions – are those of the essay on Mangan. Here Joyce defines the aesthetics of the young artist on purely symbolist grounds. But his scholastic formation leads him to retranslate his basic assumptions into Aristotelian and Thomistic terms, a seemingly superficial change but one which recasts the entire perspective.

Stephen's lecture attempts to underline the importance of a new theater and of an art free from moral preoccupations. We see here the decision to break at last with the laws and conventions of a bourgeois society. This polemic, based on a conception of the poet as creator, as founder of a new reality, originates in the essay on Mangan and is supported by a clever use of Thomistic thought.

The aesthetics of *Stephen Hero* represent this point of fusion which, developed and nuanced, will be reproposed in *A Portrait*. Although the differences between the two drafts are considerable, together they establish the main lines of an aesthetics, not lacking in rigor, in which one witnesses the amazing convergence of three diverse attitudes – realism, decadence, and the scholastic *forma mentis*.

Portrait of the Artist as a Young Thomist

The principal themes of Stephen's aesthetics are: 1) the subdivision of art into three genres – lyric, epic and dramatic; 2) the objectivity and impersonality of the work; 3) the autonomy of art; 4) the nature of the aesthetic emotion; 5) the criteria of beauty. From this last

theme emerge 6) the doctrine of the epiphany and 7) the pronounce-
ments on the nature of poetic activity and the function of the poet.

The discussion of genres is somewhat academic.[5] In the lyrical
genre the artist presents his image in immediate relationship with
himself, while in the epic he presents it in an indirect relationship
with himself and others:

> The lyrical form is in fact the simplest verbal vesture of an instant of emotion, a
> rhythmical cry such as ages ago cheered on the man who pulled at the oar or
> dragged stones up a slope. He who utters it is more conscious of the instant of
> emotion than of himself as feeling emotion (*P* 214).

On the contrary, the epic form is the continuation, almost a
maturation, of the lyrical form and assumes equidistance between
poet, reader and emotional center. The narration is no longer in first
person, and the individuality of the artist flows into the personages
like a vital sea. Joyce produces the example from the ancient ballad
Turpin Hero which begins in the first person and ends in the third.
The dramatic form is achieved:

> when the vitality which has flowed and eddied round each person fills every
> person with such vital force that he or she assumes a proper and intangible
> esthetic life. The personality of the artist, at first a cry or a cadence or a mood
> and then a fluid and lambent narrative, finally refines itself out of existence, im-
> personalizes itself, so to speak.... The mystery of esthetic like that of material
> creation is accomplished. The artist, like the God of the creation, remains within
> or behind or beyond or above his handiwork, invisible, refined out of existence,
> indifferent, paring his fingernails (*P* 215).

It is clear, at least theoretically, that the dramatic form represents
for Joyce the true and proper form of art. From such an assumption
the principle of the *impersonality* of the work of art, so typical of the
Joycean poetic, vigorously emerges. When he elaborated this theory,
Joyce had already come into contact with the analogous theories of
Mallarmé (Hayman, 1956) and certainly had in his presence the
English translation of a passage from *Crise de Vers* which bears a
noticeable resemblance to Stephen's speech:

> L'oeuvre pure implique la disparition élocutoire du poète, qui céde l'initiative
> aux mots, par le heurt de leur inégalité mobilisée; ils s'allument de reflets
> réciproques comme une virtuelle trainée de feux sur les pierreries, remplaçant la
> respiration perceptible en l'ancient souffle lyrique ou la direction personnelle
> enthousiaste de la phrase (*Oeuvres*, ed. Gallimard, p. 336).

Undoubtedly, the problem of the impersonality of the artist had already been proposed to Joyce by other youthful readings, for we can easily recognize the ancestors of this concept in Baudelaire, Flaubert, and Yeats.[6] It is necessary to recognize how widely the idea circulated throughout the Anglo-Saxon atmosphere of the epoch, later finding its definitive arrangement in the writings of Pound and Eliot.[7]

From this poetic objective, the reference to Aristotle's *Poetics* comes spontaneously. Joyce was undoubtedly influenced by the traditional Anglo-Saxon critical method of considering art in Aristotelian terms. This is demonstrated in the diversity existing between the text of *A Portrait* and the probable Mallarméan source cited above. When Mallarmé speaks of the pure artistic work in which the poet disappears, he has in mind a Platonic conception in which *l'Oeuvre* aspires to become *Le Livre*, the impersonal reflection of Beauty as an absolute essence expressed by the *Verbe*. The Mallarméan work thus tends to be an impersonal, evocative apparatus which goes beyond itself towards a world of metaphysical archetypes.[8] On the contrary, the impersonal work of Joyce appears as an object centered and resolved in itself. References are located inside the aesthetic object, and the object aspires to be the surrogate of life and not the means towards a subsequent and purer life. The Mallarméan suggestions have deep-rooted mystical ambitions while the Joycean ones aspire to be the triumph of a perfect mechanism which exhausts its own function.[9]

It is interesting to note how the Platonic conception of beauty came to Mallarmé from Baudelaire and to Baudelaire from Poe. But in Poe, the Platonic element develops according to the ways of an Aristotelian methodology which is attentive to the psychological relationship of work-reader and the constructive logic of the work (consider "The Philosophy of Composition"). Thus, starting from an Anglo-Saxon environment and the Aristotelian tradition, passing through the filter of the French symbolist poets, these and other ferments returned to Anglo-Saxon territory and were reconverted by Joyce within the ambit of an Aristotelian sensitivity.

The aesthetic formulations of St. Thomas were also influential. The quotations that Joyce had within reach nowhere discuss a work capable of expressing the personality of the poet. Joyce then realized that even Aquinas upheld the impersonal and objective work. This was not a matter of drawing a convenient conclusion from lack of contrary documents. Demonstrating a keen understanding of medieval thought, integrating the few texts with which he was acquainted, Joyce understood that the Aristotelian and Thomist aesthetics were not at all concerned with the affirmation of the artist's self: the work is an object which expresses its own structural laws and not the person of the author. For this reason, Joyce was convinced that he would not be able to elaborate a theory of the creative process on the basis of Thomist thinking. Scholasticism undoubtedly had a theory of *ars*, but this did not shed light on the process of poetic creation. Although the idea of *ars* as *recta ratio factibilium* or *ratio recta aliquorum faciendorum* could be of use to him, Joyce reduces this to a concise formula: "Art... is the human disposition of sensible or intelligible matter for an esthetic end" (*P* 207). By adding "for an esthetic end," a precision which is not considered in the medieval formula, he changes the meaning of the old definition, passing from the Greco-Latin idea of *"techne-ars"* to the modern one of *"art"* as exclusively *"fine arts."*[10] But Stephen is persuaded that his "applied Aquinas" can serve him only to a certain point: "When we come to the phenomena of artistic conception, artistic gestation and artistic reproduction I require a new terminology and a new personal experience" (*P* 209). In fact, the sporadic affirmations concerning the nature of the poet and his function that we find in *Stephen Hero* are completely foreign to the Aristotelian-Thomist problematic, as are certain allusions to the creative process in *A Portrait*.

The discourse on the autonomy of art is completely typical. Here the young Stephen reveals the formal nature of his adhesion to scholasticism. The formulas of Aquinas boldly smuggle in a theory of *l'art pour l'art* that Stephen assimilated from other sources. Aquinas affirmed that *"pulchrae dicuntur quae visa placent,"* noting furthermore that the artifex must interest himself solely in the perfection of the artistic work that he creates and not in the exterior ends to which the work can be used. But medieval theory refers to *ars* understood in a rather large sense, as the construction of objects, as handicraft, in short, as more than just the formation of works of art in the modern sense of the term. For such *ars* it establishes a standard of artisan integrity. In effect, a work of art is a form, and the perfection of a form becomes established as much in terms of *perfectio prima* as in terms of *perfectio secunda*. While the *perfectio prima* examines the formal quality of the object produced, the *perfectio secunda* considers the proper end of that object. In other words, an ax is beautiful if it is constructed according to the rules of formal harmony; but above all, it is beautiful if it is well-fitted for its final end, which is chopping wood. In the Thomist hierarchy of ends and means, the value of an object is established upon the relationship of means to ends: the entire thing is evaluated in terms of the supernatural ends to which man is oriented. Beauty, Goodness, and Truth are reciprocally implicated. Thus, a statue used for obscene or magical ends is intrinsically ugly, reflected in the sinister light of its distorted finality. To interpret the propositions of St. Thomas in a rigorously formalistic sense (as has been done by many zealous Neo-Thomists) is to misunderstand the substantially unified and hierarchial vision by which the medieval man confronted he world.[11] Therefore, when Stephen argues with the professors of the college in order to demonstrate that Aquinas "is certainly on the side of the capable artist" and when he claims not to find in Aquinas' definition of the beautiful any necessity for learning or moral elevation, Stephen conceals with casuist ability, under medieval garments, propositions like those of Wilde, for whom "all art is perfectly useless."[12] The most curious fact is that the Jesuits with whom Joyce spoke felt a certain dissatisfaction but were not in a position to object to his quotations. They were victims of their own traditional formalism in which the words of the Doctor Angelicus could not be discussed. Joyce, reversing the situation in his favor and profiting from the congenital weakness of a mental system, shows that he finds himself completely at ease with the Catholic sensitivity.

On these grounds Stephen carries forward the systematic arrangement of his aesthetics. In discussing the nature of the aesthetic emotion he is still following his conception of the autonomy of art. In aesthetic contemplation the pornographic moment is as extraneous as the didactic one. Stephen then renews ties with Aristotle, assuming the cathartic theory of poetry. He elaborates a definition of pity and terror, lamenting that Aristotle did not give a definition in the *Poetics* but ignoring it in the *Rhetoric*. Joyce defines the aesthetic emotion as a sort of stasis, the arrestment of a sensitivity before an ideal pity and terror, a stasis provoked, protracted and dissolved into what he calls the "rhythm of beauty."[13] This definition would appear to have its roots in certain modern conceptions, were it not that Stephen's definition of aesthetic rhythm is of clear Pythagorean origin:

> Rhythm . . . is the first formal esthetic relation of part to part in any esthetic whole or of an esthetic whole to its part or parts or of any part to the esthetic whole of which it is a part (P 206).

Such a definition is compared by Stuart Gilbert with an analogous one from Coleridge:

> The sense of beauty subsists in simultaneous intuition of the relation of parts, each to each, and of all to the whole: exciting an immediate and absolute complacency, without intervenence, therefore, of any interest, sensual or intellectual.[14]

Both can be related to the medieval formulation of Robert Grosseteste:

> Est autem pulchritudo concordia et convenientia sui ad omnium suarum partium singularium ad seipsas et ad se invicem et ad totum harmonia, et ipsius totius ad omnes (*Commentarium in Div. Nom.*, 88, 1).

The singularity of these three comparisons should not be surprising, for in Coleridge as in Grosseteste, there is a Platonic and Pythagorean background in which transcendentalist organicism and scholasticism join hands and converge in the formula of the young Stephen. When forced to define the essential characteristics of beauty, Stephen returns to the analogous formulations and the famous three principles stated by Aquinas. These Thomist concepts appear in the First Part (q.39, a.8) of the *Summa Theologica*:

> Ad pulchritudinem tria requiruntur. Primo quidem integritas, sive perfectio: quae enim diminuta sunt, hoc ipso turpia sunt. Et debita proportio sive consonantia. Et iterum claritas, unde quae habent colorem nitidum, pulchra esse dicuntur.

We will try to follow this interpretive process step by step. Stephen's discussion with Lynch on this topic begins with an allusion concerning the identification of beauty and truth. Here Joyce approaches the scholastic tradition, even though the metaphysical implications of the concept do not interest him:

> Truth is beheld by the intellect which is appeased by the most satisfying relations of the intelligible: beauty is beheld by the imagination which is appeased by the most satisfying relations of the sensible (*P* 208).

This definition has much in common with certain annotations added to the Thomist text, especially by commentators of the last century. The memory of certain remarks made by the professors of the college should not be excluded here. The only extraneous contribution, and in that sense curious, is the appearance of the term "imagination," absent from the medieval concept and typical of modern aesthetics. Coleridge and Poe speak of imagination; St. Thomas does not. The *visio* is not a specific faculty of the human mind but the human mind in its wholeness which focuses on the aesthetic characteristics of the object.

The notion of imagination appears in the early writings of Joyce but is not highly developed in the aesthetics of Stephen Dedalus. Here imagination is only seen as a particular relation between mind and things. As in Aquinas, it is the way the mind looks at things in order to see them aesthetically. In fact, if "The first step in the direction of beauty is to understand the frame and scope of the imagination, to comprehend the act itself of esthetic apprehension" (*P* 208), then for Stephen the frame and scope of the imagination become clarified only on the way: "all people who admire a beautiful object find in it certain relations which satisfy and coincide with the stages themselves of all esthetic apprehension" (*P* 209). Instead of explaining what the imagination is, Stephen indicates the actual process undertaken by the mind in order to grasp the sensible relations among the objects of perceptual experience. In fact, in *Stephen Hero* it is stated that "the apprehensive faculty must be scrutinised in action" (*SH* 212).[15]

The interesting fact is that while the nature of the imagination is defined in relation to the objective criteria of beauty, these criteria are defined in relation to the process undergone by the imagination in order to recognize them. This aspect of the question differentiates the Joycean attitude from that of Aquinas. In the modern author, the ontological modes of beauty become the modes of the apprehension (or production) of beauty. We will see the importance of this in the discussion of the epiphany.

In *A Portrait*, Stephen must interpret the concepts of *integritas*, *proportio*, and *claritas* which he translates by "wholeness," "harmony," and "radiance."

"Look at the basket," Stephen says to Lynch; and explains:

> In order to see that basket . . . your mind first of all separates the basket from the rest of the visible universe which is not the basket. The first phase of apprehension is a bounding line drawn about the object to be apprehended. An esthetic image is presented to us either in space or in time. What is audible is presented in time, what is visible is presented in space. But, temporal or spatial, the esthetic image is first luminously apprehended as selfbounded and selfcontained upon the immeasurable background of space or time which is not it. You apprehend it as *one* thing. You see it as one whole. You apprehend its wholeness. That is *integritas* (*P* 212).

It is clear from these lines that the Thomist *integritas* is not the Joycean *integritas*. The former is a fact of substantial completion, the latter is a fact of spatial delimitation. The former is a problem of onto-logical volume, the latter is one of physical perimeter. The Joycean *integritas* is the result of a psychological focusing; it is the imagination that selects the thing.[16]

Because the possibilities of deformation are fewer, the Joycean interpretation of the concept of *proportio* is more faithful to its Thomist counterpart than his interpretation of *integritas*:

> Then. . . you pass from point to point, led by its formal lines; you apprehend it as balanced part against part within its limits; you feel the rhythm of its structure. In other words the synthesis of immediate perception is followed by the analysis of apprehension. Having first felt that it is *one* thing you feel now that it is a *thing*. You apprehend it as complex, multiple, divisible, separable, made up of its parts, the result of its parts and their sum, harmonious. That is *consonantia* (P 212).

The remarks concerning rhythm have been explained previously. The determination of *claritas* is longer and more difficult, and the Joycean texts that refer to it are more discordant. The final drafting of *A Portrait* reads like this:

> The connotation of the word. . . is rather vague. Aquinas uses a term which seems to be inexact. It baffled me for a long time. It would lead you to believe that he had in mind symbolism or idealism, the supreme quality of beauty being a light from some other world, the idea of which the matter is but the shadow, the reality of which it is but the symbol. I thought he might mean that *claritas* is the artistic discovery and representation of the divine purpose in anything or a force of generalisation which would make the esthetic image a universal one, make it outshine its proper conditions. But that is literary talk. I understand it so. When you have apprehended that basket as one thing and have then analysed it according to its form and apprehended it as a thing you make the only synthesis which is logically and esthetically permissible. You see that it is that thing which it is and no other thing. The radiance of which he speaks is the scholastic *quiddi-tas*, the *whatness* of a thing (P 212-13).

The Joycean interpretation is quite subtle. He starts from the elemen-tary and incomplete Thomist texts, uprooted from their widest con-text, and reaches an acuteness lacking in many authorized commen-tators. As for Aquinas, the *quidditas* is the substance in so far as it can be understood and defined. Consequently, to speak about *quidditas* is to speak about substance, about form as organism and structure. In *Stephen Hero* it is said more resolutely that "The soul of the com-monest object, the structure of which is so adjusted, seems to us radiant" (*SH* 213). Here Joyce gives us an explanation that is truly congenial with Thomist thinking, without yet having extended the formulation in a personal direction. By his clear refusal of Platonic interpretations of the concept of *claritas* (when he speaks of "literary talk"), Joyce also wants to clarify his own position. In so doing, Joyce strikes the center of the issue.

Only in the passages that follow this interpretation will Stephen's discourse assume inflections of greater autonomy and thereby reveal that his fidelity to Aquinas is only a formal means by which to support a freer development of personal themes. The text from *A Portrait* reads:

> This supreme quality is felt by the artist when the esthetic image is first conceived in his imagination. The mind in that mysterious instant Shelley likened beautifully to a fading coal. The instant wherein that supreme quality of beauty, the clear radiance of the esthetic image, is apprehended luminously by the mind which has been arrested by its wholeness and fascinated by its harmony is the luminous silent stasis of esthetic pleasure, a spiritual state very like to that cardiac condition which the Italian physiologist Luigi Galvani, using a phrase almost as beautiful as Shelley's, called the enchantment of the heart (*P* 213).

In *Stephen Hero* the context is somewhat different. The moment of *radiance* comes to be defined more specifically as the moment of *epiphany*.

> By an epiphany he meant a sudden spiritual manifestation, whether in the vulgarity of speech or of a gesture or in a memorable phase of the mind itself. He believed that it was for the man of letters to record these epiphanies with extreme care, seeing that they themselves are the most delicate and evanescent of moments (*SH* 211).

The expression "fading coal" and "evanescent state of mind" are too ambiguous to be adapted to a concept like that of Thomist *claritas*. *Claritas* is the solid, clear, almost tangible display of formal harmony. Here Stephen avoids the suggestions of the medieval texts and sketches a personal theory. In *Stephen Hero* epiphany is expressly mentioned. Although the term itself does not appear in *A Portrait* (as though Joyce were cautious of the theoretical approach of his early years), the passage on the enchantment of the heart deals precisely with epiphany. What happens to the old concept of *claritas* when it is understood as "epiphany"?

Epiphany: from Scholasticism to Symbolism

The concept, not the term, "epiphany" reached Joyce from Walter Pater or, more explicitly, from that "Conclusion" to the *Studies in the History of the Renaissance* which had so great an influence on English culture between the two centuries. Rereading the pages of Pater, we realize that the analysis of the various moments in the process of the epiphanization of reality proceeds in a way that is analogous to the Joycean analysis of the three criteria of beauty. In Joyce, however, the object of analysis is a stable and objective given, while in Pater, it is the elusive flow of reality. It is not by chance that the famous "Conclusion" begins with a quotation from Heraclitus.

For Pater, reality is the sum of forces and elements that fade away as soon as they arise; they are made tangible and embodied in a troublesome presence only by our superficial experience, but when subjected to deeper reflection, they dissolve and their cohesive force is instantly suspended. We are then in a world of incoherent, flashing, unstable impressions. Habit is broken, everyday life dissolves, and only singular moments remain, seizable for an instant then immediately vanishing. In every moment, the perfection of a form appears in a hand or in a face; some tonality on the hill or on the sea is more exquisite than the rest; some state of passion or vision or intellectual excitement is "irresistibly real and attractive for us—for that moment only." Afterwards the moment has vanished, but for that moment only life has taken on a value, a reality, a reason. Not the fruit of experience, but experience itself is the end. To maintain this ecstasy would be "the success of life."

In this portrait of Pater is the English *fin de siècle* aesthete and his day-by-day strain to capture the fugitive and exquisite instant. In Joyce this heredity is purified of such delicacy and languor; Stephen Dedalus is not Marius the Epicurean. Nonetheless, the influence of the page cited above is quite vivid. Thus we realize that the entire scholastic framework that Stephen has erected to support his aesthetic perspective is used only to sustain a romantic idea of the poetic word as revelation and the poet as the only one who can give a reason to things, a meaning to life, a form to experience, a finality to the world.

Stephen's reasoning, crammed with Thomistic quotations, tends toward this resolution. In fact, only in the light of this resolution does one find real value in the various affirmations concerning the nature of the poet and the imagination that are found in Stephen's discussions and in the early writings of Joyce.

> The poet is the intense centre of the life of his age to which he stands in a relation than which none can be more vital. He alone is capable of absorbing in himself the life that surrounds him and of flinging it abroad again amid planetary music. When the poetic phenomenon is signalled in the heavens . . . it is time for the critics to verify their calculations in accordance with it. It is time for them to acknowledge that here the imagination has contemplated intensely the truth of the being of the visible world and that beauty, the splendour of truth, has been born (*SH* 80).

The poet is thus the one who, in a moment of grace, discovers the profound soul of things, and he is the one who makes them *exist* solely through the poetic word. Epiphany is thus a way of discovering reality and, at the same time, a way of defining reality through discourse. This conception develops somewhat from *Stephen Hero* to *A Portrait*. In the first book, the epiphany is still a way of seeing the world and thus a type of intellectual and emotional experience. Such experiences are represented in the sketches that the young Joyce gathers in his notebook *Epiphanies* — pieces of conversation that serve to identify a character, a tic, a typical vice, an existential experience. They are the rapid and imponderable visions that are noted in *Stephen Hero* — a conversation between two lovers overheard by chance on a foggy evening that gives Stephen "an impression keen enough to afflict his sensitiveness" (*SH* 211), or the clock in the customs which is suddenly epiphanized and, without apparent reason, becomes "important." But why, and for whom? Pater offers an answer — *for the aesthete*, at the very moment when he seizes the event at a level beyond its habitual evaluation. Various pages in *A Portrait* seem directly inspired by this idea:

> His thinking was a dusk of doubt and selfmistrust lit up at moments by the lightnings of intuition, but lightnings of so clear a splendour that in those moments the world perished about his feet as if it had been fireconsumed: and thereafter his tongue grew heavy and he met the eyes of others with unanswering eyes for he felt that the spirit of beauty had folded him round like a mantle and that in revery at least he had been acquainted with nobility.
>
> . . . .
>
> . . . he found himself glancing from one casual word to another on his right or left in stolid wonder that they had been so silently emptied of instantaneous sense until every mean shop legend bound his mind like the words of a spell and his soul shrivelled up, sighing with age as he walked on in a lane among heaps of dead language (*P* 177-79).

Sometimes the image is more rapid: the vision of the reverend Stephen Dedalus, the *Mulier cantat*, an odor of rotten cabbage. The insignificant thing takes on importance. In *Stephen Hero* these are the cases in which there seems to be a tacit agreement between the aesthete and reality. These are also the cases in which *A Portrait* most clearly shows itself as the ironic and affectionate report of those inner experiences which, in *Stephen Hero*, were the unique moments, the central moments of the aesthetic experience as identified with the experience of life.

But between *Stephen Hero* and the final draft of *A Portrait* about ten years intervene. Situated in the middle is the experience of *Dubliners*. Each short story of this collection appears like a vast epiphany, or at least the arrangements of the events tend to resolve themselves in an epiphanic experience. But it is no longer a question of a rapid and momentary note-taking, an almost stenographic relationship to life experience. Here fact and emotional experience are isolated and, through the careful strategy of narrative technique, are placed "montage-style" at the culminating part of the story where they become climax, summary, and judgment of the entire situation.

In this way the epiphanies of *Dubliners* are key moments that arise in a realistic context. They consist of common facts or phrases but acquire the value of a moral symbol, a denunciation of a certain emptiness of existence. The vision of the old dead priest in the first story, the squalid inanity of Corley with his smile of triumph while showing the little coin in "Two Gallants," the final crying of Chandler in "A Little Cloud," and the solitude of Duffy in "A Painful Case" are all brief moments that turn moral situations into metaphors as the result of an accent placed imperceptibly upon them by the narrator.

Thus, at this point in his artistic maturation Joyce seems to achieve that at which the aesthetics of *Stephen Hero* merely hinted:

> the artist who could disentangle the subtle soul of the image from its mesh of defining circumstances most exactly and "re-embody" it in artistic circumstances chosen as the most exact for it in its new office, he was the supreme artist (*SH* 78).

In *A Portrait* the epiphany is no longer an emotional moment that the artistic word helps to recall but an operative moment of art. It founds and institutes, not a way to perceive but a way to produce life. At this point Joyce abandons the word "epiphany" for it suggests a moment of vision in which *something shows itself;*[17] what now

interests him is the act of the *artist who shows something* by a
strategic elaboration of the image. Stephen truly becomes "a priest of
eternal imagination, transmuting the daily bread of experience into
the radiant body of everliving life" (*P* 221).

This affirmation acquires meaning in *Stephen Hero*, for whom the
classical style, "the syllogism of art, the only legitimate process from
one world to another," is by nature "mindful of limitations" and
"chooses rather to bend upon these present things and so to work
upon them and fashion them that the quick intelligence may go
beyond them to their meaning which is still unuttered" (*SH* 78). Art
does not record; rather, it produces epiphanic visions in order to
make the reader seize the "inside true inwardness of reality" across
the "sextuple gloria of light actually retained."

The paramount example of epiphany in *A Portrait* is that of the
seabird girl. It is no longer a question of a fleeting experience that can
be written down and communicated by brief hints. Here reality is
epiphanized through the verbal suggestions of the poet. The vision,
with all its potential for the revelation of a universe resolved in
beauty, in the pure aesthetic emotion, acquires its full importance
only in the total and unalterable structure of the page.

At this point the last suspicion of Thomism is radically discarded
and the categories of Aquinas reveal themselves as they were understood by the young artist—as a useful launching pad, a stimulating interpretive exercise whose sole purpose is to serve as the departure
point for another solution. Although the epiphanies in *Stephen Hero*,
identified with a discovery of reality, still retain a connection with the
scholastic concept of *quidditas*, the artist now builds his epiphanic
vision from the objective context of events—by connecting isolated
facts in new relationships through a completely arbitrary poetic
catalysis. An object does not reveal itself because of its verifiable, objective structure but because it becomes the symbol of an interior
moment in Stephen.

Why does it become a symbol? The object which is epiphanized
has no reasons for its epiphany other than the fact that it has been
epiphanized. Both before and after Joyce, contemporary literature
offers examples of this type. We notice that the fact is never
epiphanized because it is worthy of being epiphanized. On the contrary, it appears worthy of being epiphanized because, in fact, it *has
been* epiphanized. In pages like Montale's *Vecchi Versi*, for example,
the moth that beats against the lamp and sinks upon the table "pazza

aliando le carte" does not have any right to survival in our memory other than in the force of a fact that has survived other facts. Only after it has become *gratuitously* important can an epiphanic fact overload itself with meaning and become a symbol.

This is not an example of the revelation of a thing itself in its objective essence, *quidditas*, but the revelation of what the thing means to us in that moment. It is the value bestowed on the thing at that moment which actually *makes* the thing. The epiphany confers upon the thing a value which it did not have before encountering the gaze of the artist. In this respect the doctrine of epiphany and *radiance* is clearly in opposition to the Thomist doctrine of *claritas*. Aquinas maintains a surrender to the object and its splendor. Joyce uproots the object from its usual context, subjecting it to new conditions and conferring upon it new splendor and value as the result of a creative vision.

In this light even the *integritas* can be understood as a type of choice, a perimeter, as we have said, not so much following the contours of the given object as conferring outlines upon the chosen object. The epiphany is now the result of an art that dismantles reality and reshapes it according to new means. The evolution from the early writings, still anchored to an Aristotelian principle, to those of *A Portrait* is now complete.

Upon review of these texts in terms of the early Joycean aesthetics, we notice that in the "Pola Notebook" of 1904 Joyce again attempts to determine the phases of ordinary perception and, within it, the moment which offers the possibility of aesthetic enjoyment. Joyce thereby identifies two fundamental activities in the act of apprehension; the first is that of simple perception and the second that of "recognition" in which the perceived object is judged satisfactory and therefore beautiful and pleasing (even if it is an ugly object, it is judged beautiful and pleasing insofar as it is perceived as a formal structure). In these notes Joyce is more scholastic than he perhaps thought himself to be, posing the old question as to the "transcendental" properties of Being. He asks whether beauty is a quality that is coessential with all Being and whether every object is beautiful insofar as it is a form embodied in a determined matter and perceived through these structural characteristics — be it a flower, a monster, a moral act, a stone, a table. St. Thomas would have fully subscribed to these convictions, for which reason it is so difficult to individuate, from the point of view of Scholastic aesthetics, a specific "aesthetic" experience from the aesthetic quality of each common experience. Joyce therefore concludes that "even the most hideous object may be said to be beautiful for this reason as it is a *priori* said to be beautiful insofar as it encounters the activity of simple perception" (*CW* 147).

Joyce proposes the following solution in order to distinguish the aesthetic experience from the "normal" one: the second activity of apprehension carries a third, that of "satisfaction" in which the perceptual process is wholly fulfilled. From the intensity and duration of this satisfaction, one measures the aesthetic validity of the thing contemplated. With this, Joyce again approaches the Thomist position in which the beautiful object would be that "in cujus aspectu seu cognitione quietetur appetitus," and the fullness of aesthetic perception would consist in a sort of *pax*, a contemplative gratification. This *pax* can be easily identified with the concept of aesthetic "stasis" in the "Paris Notebook," in which Joyce resolves the Aristotelian idea of "catharsis."

Joyce takes no interest in the medico-psychological interpretation of catharsis as a Dionysiac experience, a purification effected through the kinetic stimulations of passion in order to obtain a purgation through shock. By catharsis, Joyce means the *arrest* of the feelings of pity and terror and the rising of joy. It is a rationalistic interpretation of the Aristotelian concept. At the appropriate moments, passions will be exorcized, detached from the mind of the audience and made "objective" in the pure dramatic texture of the plot. In a certain sense, these passions will be "defamiliarized" and rendered universal, thereafter "impersonal." It is understandable how Stephen Dedalus, who defends so vigorously the impersonality of art, finds himself attracted by this interpretation and makes it his own in *Stephen Hero*.

Although it appears unaltered in its surface form, the conception has radically changed from the early writings to *A Portrait*. In *A Portrait* the aesthetic joy and the stasis of passions become "the luminous silent stasis of esthetic pleasure." The terminology charges the concept with new implications. This static pleasure is not the purity of rational contemplation but the thrill in the face of mystery, the tension of sensitivity at the limits of the ineffable. Walter Pater, the symbolists, and D'Annunzio have replaced Aristotle.

In order to make this transition, Joyce needs to reconceptualize the mechanism of aesthetic perception and the nature of the perceived object. This happens in the theory of *claritas* and in the development of the idea of epiphany. Pleasure is no longer given by the fullness of an objective perception but by the subjective translation of an im-ponderable moment of experience. By a stylistic strategy, one thereby translates an actual experience into a linguistic equivalent of reality. The medieval artist was the servant of things and their laws, charged to create the work according to given rules. The Joycean art-ist, last inheritor of the romantic tradition, elicits meanings from a world that would otherwise be amorphous and, in so doing, masters the world of which he becomes the center.

Throughout *A Portrait*, Joyce thus debates a series of unresolved contradictions. Stephen, steeled in the school of the old Aquinas, re-jects both the faith and the lessons of the master, modernizing the scholastic categories by instinct, without even realizing it. He does this by drawing upon an idea that is present in contemporary culture and that deeply influenced him. This is the romantic concept of the poetic act as the foundation and resolution of the world. Through this romanticism, the world is denied as a place of objective relationships and is conceived instead as a network of subjective connections established through the poetic act.

Could this poetic theory suffice one who has absorbed the lesson of Ibsen in order to find a way of clarifying, through art, the laws that govern human events? Could it suffice someone nourished by a scholastic way of thinking, a mode of thought which is a continuous invitation to order, to clear and qualifiable structure rather than lyrical and evanescent allusion?

In other words, Joyce, who began his career of aesthete with an essay titled "Art and Life" and who found in Ibsen a profound relation-ship between the artistic work and moral experience, seems to reject any link between art and life in *A Portrait*. As his heritage of decaden-tism, he recognizes the only livable life to be the one which lives on the pages of the artist. If Joyce had stopped with *A Portrait*, nothing in the aesthetic formulation of the book could have been criticized and the aesthetics of Stephen would have been identified with those of the author. But from the moment that Joyce proposes to write *Ulysses*, he reveals the deep conviction that if art is a shaping activity, "the human disposition of sensible matter for an aesthetic end," then the exercise of shaping must be applied to a well-determined material, the tissue itself of the real events, psychological phenom-ena, moral relations, that is, to the whole of society and culture.[18] Thus Stephen's aesthetics will not entirely be the aesthetics of *Ulysses*. In fact, what Joyce states concerning *Ulysses* goes beyond the well-defined borders of the philosophical categories and the cultural choices of the young artist.

Joyce knew this and, in fact, *A Portrait* does not claim to be the aesthetic manifesto of Joyce but the portrait of a Joyce who no longer existed when the author had finished this ironic, autobiographical sketch and begun *Ulysses*. In the third chapter of the book, Stephen is walking along the beach and remembers his own youthful projects, "remember your epiphanies on green oval leaves. . . ."

Naturally, many of the major aesthetic pivots of the early Joyce remain valid in his successive works. But the aesthetics of the first two books remain exemplary under another aspect; they propose, in all its significance, the conflict between a world thought *ad mentem divi Thomae* and the need for a contemporary sensibility. This conflict will be fatally repeated in the two successive works in a different form. It is the conflict of a traditional order and a new vision of the world, the conflict of the artist who tries to give form to the chaos in which he moves yet finds in his hands the instruments of the old Order which he has not yet succeeded in replacing.

NOTES

[1] Roman Jakobson, "Closing Statements: Linguistics and Poetics," in *Style in Language*, ed. T.A. Sebek (Cambridge: MIT Press, 1960).

[2] See "The Study of Languages" (*CW*, Chapter III), in which Joyce (1898-99, at the age of sixteen) already outlines his main lines of thought: 1) the discourse must maintain "even in moments of the greatest emotion an innate symmetry"; 2) "the higher grades of language . . . are . . . the champion and exponents . . . of Truth"; 3) "in the history of words there is much that indicates the history of men." These three remarks can be read as the program of the three major works, *A Portrait*, *Ulysses*, and the *Wake*.

[3] As for Joyce's Aristotelian and Thomistic readings, see *CW*, Ellmann (1959), Noon (1957), Slocum & Cahoon (1953).

[4] In the essay on Mangan, Joyce uses an expression such as "Beauty, the splendour of truth, is a gracious presence when the imagination contemplates intensely the truth of its own being or the visible world, and the spirit which proceeds out of truth and beauty is the holy spirit of joy. These are realities and these alone give and sustain life" (*CW* 83). He here recalls a similar expression of Pater. The idea of the poet as the only saviour of mankind and the exaltation of an existence in which a "little rectitude of conduct" is matched with "poetic faculty" are typical symbolist topics. On the other hand, reference to the great cosmic memory and to the "miracle of light . . . renewed eternally in the imaginative soul" recall the various theosophical doctrines. In this perspective, even the allusion to Beauty as "splendor of the truth" loses its scholastic connotations and reflects mysteriosophic echoes.

[5] This distinction appears in Aristotle's *Poetics*, 1447 a and b to 1462 a and b. In Joyce references it appears in *SH*, Chapter XIX, and *P*, Chapter V. Noon (1957) finds a relation

with Hegel's tripartition between symbolic, classical, and romantic form and with Schelling's distinction between lyrical particularity, epic infinity and dramatic union of general and particular, real and ideal. Hegel and Schelling were certainly known by Joyce in his maturity but it is not certain that he was acquainted with them when writing the early works.

⁶ As for impersonality, see Baudelaire's "Sur Théophile Gautier"; but it seems that Joyce was not greatly influenced by this poet (in the essay on Mangan he remarks that "almost all Baudelaire is merely literature in verse"). A more profound influence seems to be that of Flaubert (see Ellmann, 1959), who has vigorously stressed the importance of impersonality ("Lettre à Mademoiselle Leroyer de Chantepie," 1857, and *Correspondence avec George Sand* [Paris: Calmann-Lévy, 1904], VII, 53). When Proust (*Les plaisirs et les jours*) speaks of Flaubert as the author who can express his vision of reality only through the use of conjunctions, he makes us think of the essay on Mangan in which great poetry is defined as "the rhythmic speech of an emotion otherwise incommunicable" (*CW* 75). As for the influence of Yeats, let us remark that the theory of the mask is nothing but the theory of the objective correlative of personality (see Wilson, 1931, on Yeats).

⁷ See, for instance, Eliot's "Tradition and the Individual Talent."

⁸ Guy Delfel, *L'esthétique de Mallarmé* (Paris: Flammarion, 1951). Against Mallarmé's poetics of "absence," Joyce holds a poetics of "presence," in which the work does not send back outside itself but sends to itself, through the mediation of concrete events and characters.

⁹ One could claim that the notion of impersonality is denied by the continuous autobiographical procedure of Joyce himself. In the article "Mr. Mason's Novels" (*CW* 130) Joyce says that Leonardo "has noted the tendency of the mind to impress its own likeness upon that which it creates"; and the entire discussion of *Hamlet* in *Ulysses* deals with the concept of the work of poetry as the image of a personal situation of its author. But it must be stressed that impersonality does not imply that the author should avoid speaking of the emotions; rather, it implies that the author must escape from the emotion, that he should not be the slave of the emotion of which he is speaking. Even the autobiography must become an objective texture of rhythms and symbols.

¹⁰ See Noon (1957, p. 28). Joyce meets the traditional definition of art by reading Aristotle and Aquinas in Paris ("Paris Notebook" and "Pola Notebook"–*CW* 143-48). Questions such as the following are typically scholastic: "Why are not excrements, children, and lice works of art? Answer: . . . The process by which they are produced is natural and non-artistic; . . . Question: Can a photograph be a work of art?" Answer: No, because it too "is a disposition of sensible matter" but not human. ". . . Question: Are houses, clothes, furniture, etc., works of art?" Answer: Yes, when "they are . . . disposed for an aesthetic end. . . ." Answers are unsatisfactory because of the rigidity of the starting definition (Joyce lacks a philosophical definition of "disposition," "matter," "human intervention") and in this sense the young artist was still too dogmatically scholastic.

¹¹ On the autonomy of art see *Summa Theologiae*, I-II, 57, 3 co; on the distinction between *perfectio prima* and *perfectio secunda* see I, 73, 1 co and 3 co; II-II, 169, 2 ad 4. On these and other topics concerning medieval aesthetics see Umberto Eco, *Il problema estetico in Tommaso d'Aquino* (1956; rpt. Milano: Bompiani, 1970), and *Sviluppo dell'estetica medievale*, in *Momenti e problemi di storia dell'estetica* (Milano: Marzorati, 1959).

[12] "[Aquinas] seems to regard the beautiful as that which satisfies the esthetic appetite and nothing more—that the mere apprehension of which pleases. . ." "But he means the sublime," the President tries to reply. And Stephen, "His remark would apply to a Dutch painter's representation of a plate of onions. . . . Aquinas is certainly on the side of the capable artist. I hear no mention of instruction or elevation" (*SH* 95-96). Stephen is casuistically manipulating *S.Th.*, I, 5, 4 and 1: "Pulchrum autem respicit vim cognoscitivam: pulchra enim dicuntur quae visa placent."

[13] According to Stephen, "Pity is the feeling which arrests the mind in the presence of whatsoever is grave and constant in human sufferings and unites it with the human sufferer. Terror is the feeling which arrests the mind in the presence of whatsoever is grave and constant in human sufferings and unites it with the secret cause" (*P* 204). According to Aristotle, "terror is a sorrow or a trouble produced by the imagining of an evil, that could arrive, bringing pain and destruction" (*Rhet.*, 1382 a) and "pity is a sorrow caused by a destructive and painful evil happening to an unmeriting person and that ourselves or somebody linked to us could expect to suffer" (*Rhet.*, 1485 b). Stephen's definitions do not differ so much from Aristotle's, except that in the place of "terror" Stephen speaks of a "secret cause" (adding a shade of romanticism to the notion of fear).

[14] *On the Principles of Genial Criticism Concerning Fine Arts*; see Gilbert (1930, p. 36).

[15] The category of imagination comes to Joyce from the romantic tradition: the term appears for the first time in the essay on Mangan and returns in the lecture on "Art and Life" (*SH*). Its romantic overtones transform the beauty, presented as the splendor of the truth, into the only possible truth. It is curious that such a romantic manipulation occurs where the young artist is praising the "classical temper." But the conversation with the President in *SH* clarifies this point: the classical temper has nothing to do with "classicism" nor with the Greek tradition; it is a more general aesthetic category and as such can be easily applied even to Mangan and other romantic poets.

[16] Noon (1957, p. 113) suggests that there is a relationship between those ideas and Berkeley's philosophy.

[17] According to Noon (1957, p. 71), the notion of epiphany came to Joyce through the interpretation of Aquinas' *claritas* proposed by De Wulf in 1895; the entire argument is based on the fact that De Wulf uses the word "epiphenomenon" in order to designate the aesthetic quality of an object. There is not, however, any proof that Joyce had read De Wulf; on the contrary, there is proof that Joyce had read D'Annunzio's *Il fuoco* (see Ellmann, 1959, pp. 60-61). The first part of *Il fuoco* is entitled "Epifania del fuoco." A term-to-term comparison between D'Annunzio's work and *A Portrait* reveals astounding stylistic and lexical affinities. See Umberto Eco, "Joyce et D'Annunzio," *L'Arc* 36 (1968), special issue on James Joyce.

[18] Cf. Goldberg (1961), namely the chapter "Art and Life."

II. Ulysses

...they say that the Demiurge tried to imitate infinite Nature which is eternal and extraneous to any limit and time of the superior
Ogdoades, but he could not reproduce its
balance and perpetuity, since he himself was
the result of a fault. Thus, in order to approach the eternity of the Ogdoades, he built
times and moments and series of innumerable years, believing to imitate, through such
an accumulation of times, the infinity of the
Ogdoades....

— Hyppolytus, *Philosophoumena*, VI, 5, 55

Joyce wanted *Dubliners* to be a "moral history" of his own country.
This same ethical and realist commitment is found in *Ulysses*, except
here, the "paralysis" of Irish life that the early novels proposed as the
primary object remains as only one of the starting points. The types
and characters of Dublin life constitute only the *literal* dimension of a
much vaster *allegorical* and *anagogical* system.

Joyce clearly thought of his novel as a *summa* of the universe:

In conception and technique I tried to depict the earth which is prehuman and
presumably posthuman (*Letters I* 180).

It is an epic of two races (Israelite-Irish) and at the same time the cycle of the
human body as well as a little story of a day (life).... It is also a sort of encyclo-
paedia. My intention is to transpose the myth *sub specie temporis nostri*. Each
adventure (that is, every hour, every organ, every art being interconnected and
interrelated in the structural scheme of the whole) should not only condition but
even create its own technique (*Letters I* 146-47).

Joyce thus conceived of a total work, a Work-as-Cosmos. The
reference point is not the poet in his ivory tower but the human com-
munity and, ultimately, all history and culture. The book is not the
journal of the artist exiled *from* the city but of everyman exiled *in* the
city. The book is also an encyclopedia and a literary *summa*: "The
task I set myself technically in writing a book from eighteen different

points of view and in as many styles, all apparently unknown or un-
discovered by my fellow tradesmen. . ." (*Letters I* 167), an undertaking which should have totally transformed culture, as it was known,
through a process of complete digestion, critical destruction, and
radical reconstruction. As he stated elsewhere, ". . . each successive
episode, dealing with some province of artistic culture (rhetoric or
music or dialectic), leaves behind it a burnt up field. Since I wrote the
Sirens I find it impossible to listen to music of any kind. . ." (*Letters
I* 129).

These are explicit, extremely ambitious programmatic statements.
Ulysses presents itself in these sentences as the uneasy crucible in
which something new is happening—the destruction of the objective
relationships sanctioned by a millenary tradition. But it is no longer
the destruction of the relationships which link a single event to its
original context in order to meld it into a new context through the
lyrical-subjective vision of the young artist. Here, the object of
destruction is larger. It is the universe of culture and, through it, the
universe *tout court*. The operation, however, is not performed on
things. It is performed *in* language, *with* language and *on* language
(on things seen through the language). Carl Gustav Jung saw this
clearly in his early review of the book and said that through a "lower-
ing of the mental level," and by the abolition of the *"fonction du réel,"*
the duality of the subjective and objective merge, bringing to light "a
being that may belong either to the physical or transcendental order."
Jung noticed that the discourse of *Ulysses* seems, at first glance, like
the monologue of a schizophrenic. But, knowing how to discern the
intentions hidden behind the writing, Jung realized that schizo-
phrenia here assumes the value of an analogical reference and
should be seen as a sort of "cubist" operation where Joyce—as all
modern artists—dissolves the image of reality in an extremely complex picture, where the tone is set by the melancholy typical of
abstract objectivity.

In this operation, warns Jung, the writer does not destroy his own
personality, as the schizophrenic, but rediscovers and establishes its
unity by destroying something else. This something else is *the classical image of the world*. "We are not facing the attack against a determined point, rather we are confronted with a universal mutation in
the spiritual texture of modern man. Doing so he clearly freed himself
from the weight of the ancient world." Thus, the book destroys
Ireland and its Middle Ages with respect to their universal signifi-

cance, a grandiose operation which necessitates the exile and the *"disparition élocutoire"* of the poet. But this impersonality, Jung reminds us, is something other than aridity. Probably, as Stephen would suggest, it is "cunning." "Under the cynicism of *Ulysses* lies a great compassion. We suffer because the world is not beautiful, is not good and, what is worse, is hopeless. We suffer because the world revolves around eternally identical days that repeat themselves over and over, pushing the human consciousness in its foolish dance through the hours, months, years" (Jung, 1932).

Jung undertakes the study of Joyce's work as though it were clinical material to analyze under the microscope, and perhaps this is the reason why Joyce never forgave him for the review. Nonetheless, the Jungian evaluations, precisely because they are free from literary biases, are among the clearest statements on the theoretical relevance of *Ulysses*. The theme of the breakage and destruction of a world, so dramatically expressed by the Swiss psychologist, is a central feature of Joyce's poetics.

The Poetics of Expressive Form

Ulysses begins with an act of rebellion, a liturgical parody, and a fireworks of destructive, scornful fraternity jokes. While in the first chapter Stephen reconfirms the crisis of religious education, in the second chapter he indicts the teachers of his civil training, the generation of well-brought-up people, the pontiffs of reactionary and philistine prejudice. Finally, in the third chapter he launches an attack against philosophy. Stephen denies the classical world not in its accidental displays but in its very nature as an orderly cosmos univocally defined by the unalterable rules of Aristotelian-Thomistic logic.

The third chapter begins with an allusion to Aristotle; the nature of the quotation, a passage from *De Anima*, is secondary.[1] What counts is the fact that Stephen begins his long walk along the beach thinking about Aristotle. But even more, he thinks *as* Aristotle. The first paragraphs of the chapter are marked by clear divisions, by rational rhythms and precise argument. Stephen is thinking about his crisis. He is no longer something, and he is not yet something else. In reflecting, he reasons like the person he was before. But gradually his eyes turn towards the sea where the figure of the drowned man is outlined. The rhythm of the monologue becomes rougher and more irregular; the ordered divisions of the topics become an uninterrupted flow in which things and ideas lose their physiognomy and appear confused, ambiguous and two-faced. At this point, the tone of the monologue justifies the reference to Proteus, the Homeric title of the chapter. It is not so much the content but the form of Stephen's thoughts which signals the passage from an orderly cosmos to a fluid and watery chaos. Here death and rebirth, the outlines of objects, human destiny itself become amorphous and pregnant with possibility. This is "Proteus," a universe in which new connections are established among things. Proteus thus takes us to the center of *Ulysses* and provides the basis of a world dominated by metamorphoses which continuously produce new centers of relations. As has been said, "Proteus" dissolves Aristotelian philosophy into a sea music.[2]

"Proteus" is a declaration of poetics, even though the poet says nothing about his work. In fact, the chapter accomplishes its programmatic declarations not by its explicit contents but by the form of the text. "Proteus" establishes the *possibility of a book whose form will be the principal and most explicit of its messages*. If we follow the various revisions of *Ulysses*, we see that the work evolves in the direction of what has been called "expressive form": the form of the chapter or the word itself conveys its subject matter.[3]

While it could be said that in all works of art a form "expresses" its content, in pieces of literature, the content is often an explicit judgment that is presented in a neutral, stylized form. For example, when Dante wants to express his disdain for the paralysis of Italian politics and, alternately, his compassion for the tender love of Paolo and Francesca, he formulates two different moral judgments (content) and expresses both of them through a single form, the stylized frame of the tercet. In this case there is no relationship between the neutral form of the tercet and the explicit judgment which is its content.

By contrast, when Joyce wants to denounce the paralysis of Irish life and, in turn, the paralysis and disintegration of the world in the chapter "Aeolus," his judgment does not appear as an explicit "content" of the text. Rather, it is represented solely by the form of the chapter, in which all the rhetorical figures are employed. Joyce does nothing but record the vacuous and presumptuous exchanges of newsmen without pronouncing judgment. The various phases of discussion are divided into paragraphs titled as journalistic news, a progressive review of the style of journalistic titling—from the Victorian newspaper to the daily evening news—from the classical title to its slang counterpart.

This radical conversion from "meaning" as content of an expression, to the form of the expression as meaning, is the direct consequence of the refusal and destruction of the traditional world in *Ulysses*. When a "lump" of experience is dominated by a univocal, stable vision of the world, it can be expressed by words that are explicit judgments on what is said. But when the material of experience assails us without our possessing its interpretive framework—when we notice that the codes of interpretation can be different, more open, flexible, and full of possibilities, and yet we still don't have the key for using them—then experience must *show itself* directly in the word.

Experience therefore "speaks" by itself and the form that it assumes speaks by itself. This form is still the old one, for rhetorical figures of speech are handed down from a linguistic heritage. The writer does not invent them but finds these figures as instruments of common use. Nevertheless, in putting them together violently, in reducing experience to formulas that for centuries have been used, worn out and cast into empty forms, the writer brings these assumptions to judgment. He lets experience incorporate itself into its customary linguistic garb, and by this incriminating movement the experience is unveiled and recognized as false.

At this point, the illusion of "judging" by means of instruments irreparably committed to upholding the social and cultural situations being described would only be an instance of "false conscience." In contrast, to judge by mere "ostension" is not perhaps the best solution, but it keeps the material free from ideological schemas and preserves it as immediate and brutal evidence.

This form of the story becomes a revelatory image of an entire situation and is, using the categories of Stephen Dedalus, an epiphany. But it is not an epiphany-*vision*; it is an epiphany-*structure*. This reduction of the judgments of the author to the pure self-manifestation of the expressive form is the highest realization of the "dramatic" and "classical" ideals proposed in the early works. While the traditional novel is invested with the point of view of an omniscient author who penetrates the soul of the characters, explaining, defining, and judging them (doing the same with things, objects, and natural events), the "dramatic" technique eliminates the continuous presence of the author and substitutes for his point of view that of the characters and the events themselves. Modern journalism is told from the point of view of modern journalism; the noises around Bloom are perceived as Bloom would perceive them; Molly's passions are defined as Molly, in suffering them, would define them.

The author standing behind or beyond or above this handiwork is not indifferent, paring his fingernails, for he takes the point of view of the characters. He translates himself into objective form. Flaubert, for example, asserts that he has interjected none of his feelings into Madame Bovary but also states, "Madame Bovary, c'est moi." In fact, after Flaubert, after James, and definitely after Joyce, contemporary narratives assume this impersonal-dramatic ideal. The author no longer speaks himself nor does he make the characters speak of themselves. Rather, he makes the way in which the characters speak and the way in which things appear to them expressive. This, in fact, is the technique that cinema has used since its very beginnings. In the *Battleship Potemkin* Eisenstein does not "judge" the relationship of crew to machine but shows his judgment in a convulsed editing of images of the machine and the machinists tied to it, virtually identified with its movements. This is also true of Godard in *A Bout de Souffle*, a film which recounts the story of a lost and alienated youth. Godard edits the film, and therefore the mode of seeing things, in the same way as its lost and alienated protagonist would see. He violates relationships of time and space, rendering the rhythms and the position of the camera improbable. The editing of the director *is* the protagonist's way of thinking.

The Poetics of the "Coupe en Largeur"

In order to bring to a close this project of dramatic narration, Joyce must above all dissolve, with the object of his narration, the instrument, the very structure of the "well made" novel which characterized it until the beginning of the century. In place of the poetics of the plot, he must substitute the poetics of the *coupe en largeur*. The poetics of the "well made" novel has its roots in the Aristotelian poetic, in the norms that were given by Aristotle for the construction of a tragic plot. While history, daily life, is a complex of disordered events which occur over a period of time, poetry, art in general, establishes among this complex of facts a logical thread, a necessary sequence in which some events are chosen and some overlooked according to requirements of verisimilitude. This is the principle of the traditional novel, what Maupassant announced in the introduction to *Pierre et Jean*:

> La vie... laisse tout au même plan, précipite les faits ou les traîne indéfiniment. L'art, au contraire, consiste à user des précautions et des préparations...à mettre en pleine lumière, par la seule adresse de la composition, les événements essentiels et à donner à tous les autres le degré de relief qui leur convient, suivant leur importance....

Here Maupassant gives the rules of a realistic narrative, capable of showing life as it is. But even in this case, he does not violate the main rule of the traditional novel; a criterion of "necessity" must link only the *important* events:

> S'il fait tenir dans trois cents pages dix and d'une vie pour montrer quelle a été, au milieu de tous les êtres qui l'ont entouré, sa signification particulière et bien caractéristique, il devra savoir éliminer, parmi les menus événements innombrables et quotidiens, tous ceux qui lui sont inutiles, et mettre en lumière, d'une façon spéciale, tous ceux qui seront demeurés inaperçus pour des observateurs peu clarvoyants....

The traditional novel must disregard, for example, the fact that the protagonist blew his nose, unless the act means something from the point of view of the necessity of the plot. The act which does not "mean" is an insignificant and therefore a "stupid" one. With Joyce, we have the full acceptance of all the stupid acts of daily life as narrative material. The Aristotelian perspective is radically overturned. What was first inessential becomes the center of the action. Important things no longer happen in the novel, but an assortment of little things, without order, in an incoherent flow—thoughts and gestures, psychic associations as well as behavior automatisms.

This renouncement of the hierarchical organization of facts means eliminating the traditional conditions for judgment. In the "well made" novel the judgment exists by virtue of the plot. A plot proposes causal connections and thus explanations; it states that fact B happens because of fact A. When one tells a story using this narrative convention, one pretends *to tame history*. According to Aristotle, it is a question of eliminating the fortuitousness of "history" (the mere presence of *res gestae*) and joining it to the perspective of "poetry" (the organization of a *historia rerum gestarum*). On the contrary, *Ulysses* offers the choice of the *res gestae* against the *historia rerum gestarum*, of life against poetry, the indiscriminate use of all the events, the renouncing of choice, the leveling of the insignificant fact next to the fact that counts. No fact is more or less significant than another fact; they all become weightless for they all have the same importance. In *Ulysses* the ambitious project expressed by Eduard in the *Faux Monnayeurs* is realized:

> Mon roman n'as pas de sujet. Oui, je sais bien; ça a l'air stupide ce que je dis là. Mettons si vous préférez qu'il n'aura pas *un* sujet. . . . Une "tranche de vie" disait l'école naturaliste. Le grand défaut de cette école c'est de couper sa tranche toujours dans le même sens du temps, en longueur. Pourqoi pas en largeur? ou en profondeur? Pour moi, je voudrais en pas couper du tout. Comprenez-moi: je voudrais tout y faire entrer, dans ce roman. Pas de coup de ciseaux pour arrêter, ici plutôt que là, sa substance. Depuis plus d'un an que j'y travaille il ne m'arrive rien que je n'y verse, et que je n'y veuille faire entrer: ce que je vois, ce que je sais, tout ce que m'apprend la vie des autres et la mienne (*Faux Monnayeurs*, II, 3).

But Eduard's poetics, even if clearly expressed, arrives too late, not only after Joyce's work but also after an established trend of contemporary fiction and psychology which converged, before Joyce, in the poetics of the *interior monologue*. The notion of a stream of consciousness is proposed in 1890 in William James' *Principles of Psychology*. In the preceding year Bergson's *Essai sur les données immediates de la conscience* appeared, and in 1905 Proust began the *Recherche*. These events opened discussion on the problem of inner experience as a continuous flow, as an amalgam of experiences as James describes it, as the invisible progress of a past that bites into the future, to repeat the Bergsonian metaphor. Nonetheless, from the very first the novelists themselves anticipated the research in psychology and philosophy and posed the problem of experience that cannot be reduced to narrative simplifications. In 1880, with the intervention of Robert Louis Stevenson, Henry James and Walter Besant debated the nature of the novel. Besant asserted that while life is "monstrous, infinite, illogical, abrupt and spasmodic," a work of art must be "clear, finite, self-contained, fluid." James, however, argued:

> Humanity is immense, and reality has a myriad forms, the most one can affirm is that some of the flowers of fiction have the odour of it, and others have not; as for telling you in advance how your nosegay should be composed, that is another affair. It is equally excellent and inconclusive to say that one must write from experience; to our suppositious aspirant such a declaration might savour of mockery. What kind of experience is intended, and where does it begin and end? Experience is never limited, and it is never complete; it is an immense sen-

sibility, a kind of huge spider-web of the finest silken threads suspended in the chamber of consciousness, and catching every airborne particle in its tissue. It is the very atmosphere of the mind; and when the mind is imaginative – much more when it happens to be that of a man of genius – it takes to itself the faintest hints of life, it converts the very pulses of the air into revelation.[4]

These statements by James seem closer to the theories of the young Stephen than to the poetics of *Ulysses*. The quoted debate fits into the artistic curriculum of James between *The American* (1877) and the later novels, which increasingly clarify the poetics of *point of view*. The technique of *point of view* is the transferring of the action of exterior facts to the mind of the characters, the disappearance of an omniscient narrator (thus the first step towards the "dramatic" impersonality of the God of the creation), and the opening of a narrative universe that can be seen in different ways, assuming diverse and complementary meanings.

Joyce thus confronts the composition of *Ulysses* after the terms for the technique of the *coupe en largeur* and the stream of consciousness have been established by literary tradition. This does not diminish the importance of his solution because Joyce's work is the first to clearly utilize the possibilities of such operative decisions. It permits us to single out the elements of his poetics and to locate them within a tradition that Joyce fully accepts.

It is along these lines that Joyce, in the use of the *stream*, seeks to hold onto and to show us a life "split in the middle," where all the conscious and unconscious ferments are swarming in the mind of the character. Until then, the world was communicated to us in explicit terms which were submitted to the censure of the consciousness. With the interior monologue, Joyce destroys his traditional image of the world. He does not, however, give himself over to collecting the fragments of a world already destroyed or still shapeless. In fact, one of the most obvious objections to the theory of the stream of consciousness is that it is not the registration of *all* the psychological events of a character, but the fruit of the author's selection. Thus, in the last analysis it is a return to the poetics of the plot, even if based on other criteria of choice.

Basically this is true. The Joycean stream of consciousness is the effort of a patient and careful handicraft. The objection is valid, however, only if one thinks that the relationship between the novel and reality is a relation of imitation. But such naiveté was not even displayed by the ancients, who agreed that *ars imitatur naturam* but added *in sua operatione*, meaning by this that art reproduces nature by the imitation of its formative processes and therefore becomes an equivalent of nature (a point that, according to the "Paris Notebook" [*CW*], Joyce understood quite well).

The internal monologue can be said to effectively register the *whole* of the stream of consciousness if one accepts the reduction of verifiable reality to that which is said by the artist. This presupposes the identification between the real universe and the work of art, a narrative convention that is essential for understanding Joycean poetics. The stream of consciousness technique has all the appearances of the most decisive naturalistic, realistic reduction, and yet it achieves a life-language identification that is derived from symbolist poetics. At the same time, it claims to reduce the real universe into the verbal sphere of an immense encyclopedia, a *summa* which is still unequivocally medieval. Once again the various poetics of Joyce are in play — realism, symbolism, medievalism.

The Poetics of the Ordo Rhetoricus

Along with the plot structure and the traditional criterion of narrative choice, the vision of time is fragmented in *Ulysses*. A classical plot presupposes a vision of the past from the point of view of the eternity that can measure it. Only an omniscient observer can instantly gather from a given fact both its remote antecedents and its future consequences. Only in this way can the fact be established as significant in the final chain of causes and effects. By contrast, in *Ulysses*, time is experienced as change but *from within*. The reader and the author move towards a possession of time from inside the flow. If there is a law of the historical process, it cannot be found outside the process itself, for the option is already determined from the individual point of view one holds within *the process* (see Meyerhoff, 1955).

But if we move *inside* the facts of consciousness and if each fact is recorded with the same absolute fidelity as any other, then personal identity falls into doubt. In the flow of perceptions during Bloom's walk along the streets of Dublin, the boundaries between "inside" and "outside" become extremely vague. Since individual consciousness is reduced to an anonymous screen that registers the stimuli that bombard it from all directions, the thoughts of one personage can be thought by another a few chapters later. In the open sea of the *stream of consciousness* one finds no individual minds that think the events but only events flowing in uniform distribution which are gradually thought by someone. In the end, the totality of the events thought will constitute a recognizable, organized field and thus a substitute for the fictional "consciousness" that has thought them.

This situation brings to mind many discussions in contemporary psychology and epistemology. The problems that the novelist confronts in using such techniques are analogous to those that the philosopher encounters in redefining the concept of "personality," "individual consciousness," "perceptual field," etc. By decomposing thought and thus the traditional entity "mind" into the sum of individual "thoughts," the author faces both a crisis in narrative time and a crisis of the personage.

This problem emerges, however, only if we take the author's point of view in the construction of his sequences. From the reader's point of view the problem is easier. From the very moment that we are familiar with the narrative technique of *Ulysses*, we are able to isolate the various personages in the magma of voices, figures, ideas, and odors that constitute the general field of events. Not only do we individuate Bloom, Molly and Stephen, but we also manage to characterize and judge them. The reason is quite simple. Each personage is constituted by the same undifferentiated field of physical and mental events, yet each is united by a personal style of discourse. Bloom's stream assumes characteristics diverse from Stephen's and Stephen's stream differs from that of Molly. As the result of these stylistic solutions, the personages of *Ulysses* appear more alive, more complex and more individualized than those of any good traditional novel in which an omniscient author pauses to describe and explain every internal event of his hero.

The problem is quite different from the operative point of view of the artist. As a reader, we succeed in connecting two mentally dissociated events and in recognizing that both belong to Bloom; we attribute this possibility to the efficient operation of a stylistic structure. But how does this structure function? Joyce accepts a dissolution of the traditional concept of the individual consciousness yet restores to us the personage-consciousnesses. In doing this, and resolving a series of problems that are current to philosophical anthropology, he utilizes certain techniques of cohesion that must be individuated. In isolating these techniques, we realize that even here the author has elaborated new coordinates of the personality, reflecting his taste for compromise, and that he has supported these new anthropological dimensions by skillfully introducing old schemas into a new context.

It is said that no one commits a crime in *Ulysses* because passion is lacking—and passion alone is the motive of every narrative machine. But might not the humiliation of the wandering and betrayed Bloom, his desperate need for paternity be defined as passion? We must ask why we are able to single out these "emotive markers" in the character of Bloom without losing ourselves in the sea of mental events distributed almost statistically and with equal emphasis. These emotive markers become clear if each gesture of the personage and those around him, each word, each mental event, the very form and operative technique of the work is seen in reference to a system of coordinates. This system permits the identification of connecting nodes from within a spacial-temporal continuum in which everything has the initial right of associating with everything.

The problem of these coordinates is the central problem of the poetics of *Ulysses* and is, once again, the problem of art as Stephen conceives it. If art is the human way to organize sensible or intelligible material for an aesthetic purpose, then the artistic problem of *Ulysses* is the accomplishment of an *order*. This may seem paradoxical, for *Ulysses*, according to Jung, is the book that proceeds to destroy the world. Similarly, E.R. Curtius (1929) notes a metaphysical nihilism at the root, where macrocosm and microcosm are fused in the void, while human culture bursts into flames turning to ashes as if in a cosmic holocaust. Richard Blackmur (1948) mentions that unlike Dante, who gives order to things, Joyce presents a type of nihilism in an irrational order. From these examples, one might suppose that the essence of the book is the declaration of disorder.

But the paradox is a structural one: in order to make disorder detectable, the author must give a shape to confusion and destruction. The problem of *Ulysses* is to find the form of disorder. Joyce faces the task of translating the magma of experience to the printed page with absolute realism. Thus Joyce finds himself before Erebus and the Night, the underground powers unleashed from their origins, the curse of five thousand years of culture encrusted on each movement, each word. He wishes to give us the image of a world in which multiple events jostle against one another, attract and repel each other, as in a statistical distribution of subatomic events, thus allowing the reader to design multiple perspectives of the "Work-Cosmos."

In fact, the book is a sum of cultural references—Homer, Theosophy, Theology, Anthropology, *Corpus Hermeticum*, Ireland, the

Catholic liturgy, the kabbala, memories of scholasticism, daily events, psychic processes, gestures, sabbatical illusions, the ties of blood and parenthood, physiological processes, odors and tastes, noises and apparitions. The possibilities for symbolic relationships among these cultural references are not those of the medieval Cosmos in which each creature becomes the "sign" of something else on the grounds of the univocal code of the *Bestiary* and the *Lapidary*, the *Encyclopedia* and the *Imago Mundi*. In the medieval symbol, the signifying-signified relationship is clear because of a homogenous culture. This homogeneity of a unique culture is lacking in the contemporary poetic symbol as the result of a multiplicity of cultural perspectives. In the contemporary symbol, signifier-signified are joined in a short circuit which is poetically necessary but ontologically gratuitous and improvised. The organizing key to this circuit does not rely upon an objective code lying outside of the work but upon an internal set of relationships which are embedded in its structure. The "Work as Cosmos" reproposes, ex novo, the linguistic conventions upon which it stands as the key to its own code. When Jean de Meung fills the *Roman de la Rose* with symbolic figures and emblems, he has no need to explain what he is talking about for his contemporaries knew. Eliot, on the other hand, must write a series of notes to *The Wasteland*, citing Frazer, Miss Weston, and the Tarots— and not even at this point can one move easily throughout his message.

To record the totality of the symbolic possibilities that criss-cross one another in all dimensions of the contemporary cultural universe is the desperate task in which Joyce, no longer Stephen, feels the terror of Chaos. Stephen wrote on the front page of his geography book in the Clongowes Wood College: "Stephen Dedalus—Class of Elements—Clongowes Wood College—Sallins—County Kildare—Ireland —Europe—The World—The Universe." The places whose names he had to learn "were all in different countries and the countries were in continents and the continents were in the world and the world was in the universe" (P 15). It was a child's discovery of that *Ordo* in which the peaceful consciousness of the medievals was founded and whose fall coincided with the birth of modern sensitivity. In the moment in which he renounces family, country and church, Stephen knows he is renouncing the Cosmos in order to participate in the business of contemporary man: to rearrange the world according to the measure of his own situation. His recollection of the Order of Clongowes

Wood is seductive, but the possibility of cultivating a new world from a Chaos challenges him to break new ground.

At this point Joyce assumes the decision of an old and hardened schoolman "steeled in the school of the old Aquinas" and brings the taste for compromise, inherited from the Jesuit masters, into the heart of his formative acts. With the same sovereign disinterest, the genius for formalism, the irreverent and unfair familiarity with the *auctoritates* that marks the good commentators of the schools of medieval theology (always ready to find in Saint Chrysostom or in Saint Jerome an expression adequate to justify the philosophical solution that appears to be most reasonable), Joyce asks the authority of the medieval Order to guarantee the existence of the new world that he has discovered. Here, in the magma of the experience brought to light through the *coupe en largeur*, he superimposes a net of traditional orders, a web of selective grills and proportional frames like those that were used by the ancient sculptors and architects in order to establish the symmetrical points of their constructions. These general schemas support a discourse built upon a hierarchy of arguments and a number of correspondences. A similar schema can be found in the *Summa Theologiae*, with its subdivisions of the genealogical tree in which God is considered as the Exemplary Cause, both in himself and in relationship to the creatures for whom he is seen as Efficient, Final and Restoring Cause. Each one of these subdivisions branches into an examination of the creation of the angels, the world, and man, so as to arrive at the definition of acts, passions, habits and virtues, and finally to the study of the mystery of incarnation, to the sacraments as continuous instruments of redemption and to death itself as the vestibule of Eternal Life. This is the organizing grill that insures that no *quaestio* appear by chance and that even the most banal arguments (feminine beauty, the lawfulness of makeup, or the excellence of the sense of smell in resurrected bodies) have their own function within the whole.

These characteristics of an organism arranged according to the most rigorous criteria of a traditional formalism are found in that reverse *Summa* which is *Ulysses*. Each chapter corresponds to an hour of the day, an organ of the body, an art, a color, a symbolic figure, and each uses a distinctive stylistic technique. The first three chapters are dedicated to Stephen, the twelve central ones to Bloom and the last three to the Stephen-Bloom meeting. These final chapters become tighter and more definitive as a result of the last chapter, dominated by Molly, in which the possibility arises of an adulterous triangle which might unite the three in the future. Into this triangle another scheme is inserted, leading the reader to identify the three persons with those of the Holy Trinity.

With this reference frame,[6] we realize that Joyce is fully assuming that medieval *forma mentis* and the "scholastic" poetics from which Stephen believes to have liberated himself with his act of rebellion. The three Thomist criteria of beauty return to the scene, and the medieval *proportio* serves to orient the correspondences. The interpretation given by T.S. Eliot (1923) is still valid: Joyce refuses the substance of the scholastic *ordo* and accepts the chaos of the contemporary world, but he attempts to reduce its apories within the form of the *ordo* that was rejected. All of this is accomplished by the use of proportional modules of a typically medieval origin. For this reason, with *Ulysses* we can speak of the continuous application of a type of historically recognizable *proportio*, that of the *artes rhetoricae*, the rule of the well-constructed discourse according to the principle of divine creation. Mathieu de Vendôme or Geoffroy de Vinsauf, theorists of the poetry of the twelfth century, would have been happy with the iron-clad rules that support the discourse of *Ulysses*.

The structure of this discourse has been compared to the sonata form. It branches into three parts, the first and the third containing three chapters each. The first part introduces and develops the theme of Stephen. The second introduces the theme of Bloom and leads it to intersect with the theme of Stephen through a polyphonic structure. The third part concludes the two themes in a symphonic recapitulation of Molly's monologue. *Ulysses* accomplishes that *consonantia*, that *unitas varietatis*, that *apta coadunatio diversorum* which constitutes, for the scholastic mind, the essential condition of beauty and aesthetic pleasure, *sicut in sono bene harmonizato*.

The eleventh chapter, that of the "Sirens," with its musical structure, its polyphonic overlapping of narrative themes, and its narrative disposition of sounds and noises, conveys the most developed musical sensibilities of the work. The identification of the musical aesthetic with an aesthetic of proportion was present throughout the entire Middle Ages, for in the Pythagorean tradition music is the symbolic figure of aesthetic phenomena. The medieval theoreticians orchestrated an immense interplay of relations between micro- and macrocosm — in the pages of Boetius, in the commentaries, in

Dionysius the Areopagite. Similarly, the eighteen chapters of *Ulysses* that refer to the various parts of the human body are ultimately united into the image of a single body that appears in cosmic scale as the symbol of the Joycean universe. Every episode performs one possible narrative technique, while the central episode, "Wandering Rocks," in its eighteen paragraphs, reproduces the techniques of the eighteen major chapters, in a minor scale.

It is indeed a *universitas in modo cytharae disposita in qua diversa rerum genera in modo chordarum sint consonantia* which appeared to Honorius of Autun as the image of the world.[7] It is the complete and complex fulfillment of the *ornatus facilis* and of the *ornatus difficilis*, of the *ordo naturalis* (beginning, middle, end) and of the *ordo artificialis* (reversing of the sentence, beginning from the end, or from the middle, or from any point—with a peculiar affinity to the processes of overturning and "cancrization" used for the dodecaphonic series) which we find recommended in the *Poetria Nova* of Geoffroy de Vinsauf and which are typical of those medieval rhetoricians of whom Faral says, "They knew for example what effects to draw from the symmetry of the scenes forming a diptych or triptych, from a story full of suspense, from the connecting of various plots conducted simultaneously."[8]

With this dense plot of artifices, the author of *Ulysses* obtains all that the medieval poet would have hoped to achieve with the same methods. Joyce creates a story interwoven with symbols and ciphered allusions, with "winks" from one scholarly intelligence to another, for under the "Velame delli versi strani" lies an ulterior reality, and each word, each image not only points to one thing but, at the same time, indicates another.

> Omnis mundi creatura
> quasi liber et pictura
> nobis est in speculum
> nostrae vitae, nostrae mortis,
> nostri status, nostrae sortis,
> fidele signaculum[9]

It is essentially the medieval nature of the work that generates its symbolic effectiveness and provides not only a literal but a moral, allegorical, and anagogical sense. We have the odyssey of Everyman exiled in a daily and unknown world, and we have the allegory of modern society and the world reflected in the history of a city. Beyond the human city, we have reference to the Heavenly City, a second order sense, an allusion to the Trinity. In the medieval poem, this secondary sense relies upon the literal sense and constitutes the ultimate end of the story. In *Ulysses* this situation is reversed, for the Heavenly City serves as the means for interpreting the literal sense. In other words, the celestial references give direction and body to the concrete, literal events. The Trinitarian schema becomes a tool which we use in order to interpret the literal level and to give meaning to the turmoil of events that explodes before our eyes. The means-end relationship is diabolically inverted.

Once again, Joyce does not use traditional narrative structures and linguistic techniques to express and connect new ideas. Rather, he takes old ideas, sanctioned by a cultural tradition, and derives new linguistic connections and narrative structures from them. The adaptation of the Trinitarian schema is a typical example of an ancient schema, a theology that Joyce does not accept, freely adapted in order to dominate a material that escapes him.[10]

While *Dubliners* expresses a situation of "paralysis," *Ulysses* expresses a demand for integration. The starting point is a lack of relations. Stephen has refused his religious universe, family, country, and church, seeking something that he does not yet know. He is in the same condition as Hamlet. He has lost a father and does not recognize any established authority; he has refused to pray for his own dying mother. Now he is oppressed by remorse for having done what he had to do. He does not even believe in the diagnosis of his own disintegration. Stephen spends two hours trying to analyze the father-son relationship both in Hamlet and in the personal life of Shakespeare (an analysis that will be used by many interpreters of *Ulysses* who search for a key to the schema of the work). But when Stephen is asked if he believes the theories he has exposited, he *promptly* replies "no." Bloom, in turn, is deprived of a true relation with the city because he is a Jew, with his wife because she betrays him, and with his son because Rudy is dead. He is the father who searches for himself in his son, and at the same time, he is Ulysses without a country. Molly, finally, would like to unite herself with the entire world, but the fulfillment of her wishes is blocked by her laziness and the pure carnality of all her relationships.

The situation expresses a total dissociation. This divided world recognizes itself as such but does not succeed in finding internal patterns of organization. This is why Joyce resorts to an external form. He makes his story the strange allegory of the Trinitarian mystery, a father that can recognize himself only in his son, a son that finds himself, or will find himself, only in relation to the father, a third person who fulfills the relationship through a caricature, an overturning of the divine, consubstantial love.[11] Even here, whoever would try to bring the parallel to its extreme limits and locate a subtle and verifiable correspondence in each event would be deluded. Once again Joyce demonstrates his use of cultural data to make, above all, a "music of ideas." He approaches ideas, shows connections, plays on references but does not make philosophy. The Trinitarian schema is used to give an order to this play of mirrors and to shape an infinite regress of references into an external frame. As this frame is rigid, it challenges the endless mobility of experiences and thereby creates a permanent dialectical movement.

Consequently, in certain moments one could be tempted to ask if order really functions as a referential frame for the reader, or if it is not simply an operative structure useful to the writer in the construction of the work but discardable once the work is finished. The same argument is advanced by art scholars who claim that the interplay of thrusts and counterthrusts in the gothic cross-vault served more in supporting the various phases of construction than in stabilizing the finished building.

If one follows Joyce during the formation of *Ulysses* and through the subsequent editing of the text, one recognizes that the order effectively served the author by helping to organize material that otherwise would have escaped him. The fact that Joyce chose not to include the references to the various chapters of the *Odyssey* within the titles of his chapters suggests that these references served during the growth of *Ulysses*, not to the *Ulysses* grown and finished. Order was to be so deeply embedded within the narrative material that the reader need only respond rather than analyze it. Nonetheless, each attempt to explain symbols and actions in *Ulysses* forces us to turn to the mediations of Gorman or Stuart Gilbert for information as to the use of the Homeric models. This indicates that the internal order has value as an external frame from which to decipher the work, a key to interpretation. The code must accompany the message, not because the message is obscure, but because the message considers even the code as one of its contents.

One might say that order serves above all as a "cartoon" of the mosaic that Joyce assembles, piece by piece, sometimes not in sequence but in such a way that the basic design guides his operation even if it is destined to disappear. But order is not only a departure point; it is also a point of arrival. In fact it is well known that many of the technical devices by which each episode fits a schema of the various correspondences of the arts or the parts of the human body were introduced at the end of the writing process. This suggests that these schematic correspondences were not only an operative means to liquidate at the end but one of the results to attain.[12]

In reality, the two aspects are complementary. Following the revisions of a passage, we realize that Joyce proceeds by augmenting the sum of allusions with repetitions of leitmotiv and with references to other apparitions in other chapters. All of these elements serve to reinforce the general schema of the correspondences, to thicken the plot of cross-references. Thus, the general picture allows this proliferation of elements, and these proliferating elements reconfirm the picture and help it to emerge with greater visibility.

With the acceptance and recognition of these modules of order, one enters easily into the world of *Ulysses*. One now possesses the thread of Ariadne, ten compasses, a hundred different topographical plans. It is possible to enter into this polyhedric Dublin, as into a house of mysteries or a palace of mirrors, and to move with ease. The knowledge that Molly has a role in the Trinitarian schema, that according to the anthropological line she is Demeter or Gea Tellus, that along the abscissa of the Greek myth she is to be identified with Penelope, does not prevent access to the individual Molly, nor does it prevent one from recognizing her as a universal type. Only at this point can one coordinate the perceptive flow of the personage and isolate the nuclei of intentions and meanings. Only then, surrounded by rigid schemas, as in a museum of wax figures, by intellectual and over-cultured references which would be capable of killing any character created by any writer, the humanity of the personage emerges — her unsatisfied desolation, the glory and squalor of her carnality, the enfolding immensity of her telluric femininity.

While symbols and allegories exist in a medieval poem in order to give sense to the Ordo that they are trying to define, in *Ulysses* the Ordo serves to give sense to the symbolic relations. It would be dangerous to refuse the Ordo as if it were the intellectual whim of the interpreter. The book would weaken, waste itself, lose any communicative power.

The Symbolic Correspondences

The contemporary world, of which *Ulysses* is both mirror and figure, lacks those conditions of unity among the various symbolic discourses that were the basic conditions of medieval symbolism. But the suggestion, the code, and the allusion become understandable, even when used subjectively, because of the general framework of the medieval theory of Order. When Joyce tells Frank Budgen that he would like the reader to understand by means of suggestion and not by means of direct statement, he refers explicitly to the dictates of a Mallarméan poetics. These suggestions are based upon a series of stylistic devices that have a great affinity with those of symbolism: phonic analogies, onomatopoeias, rapid associations of ideas, and finally, true and proper symbols. None of these symbols, however, rests upon the pure evocative magic of the word, the sound, the white space around the phrase as it was with Mallarmé. The device "functions" if the suggestive element possesses a "direction," if the suggestion finds support in the general schema. By "direction" we do not mean "univocity." The referential schema does not transform the suggestion into a reference. The sign remains ambiguous, endowed with multiple meanings. Nevertheless, the referential schema provides a field of suggestion, framing it in a series of possible directions.

Recall the two examples proposed by Joyce in his confidences to Frank Budgen. When approaching the restaurant, the hungry Bloom thinks of his wife's legs and mentally notes, "Molly looks out of plumb." Now, cautions Joyce, there were many ways of formulating the thought, but to Bloom the word "plumb" comes to mind, a word which suggests "plum." Actually, it wasn't necessary for Joyce to advise us of this reference, for the chapter in which Bloom formulates this thought is riddled with a series of onomatopoeias that recall the acts of nutrition, mastication, swallowing, and playing with food. All the thoughts deal with food. "Monday," a few paragraphs ahead, will appear as "munchday"; the "plum" concealed in "plumb" appears in the advertising slogan of the meat dough, Plumtree.

These references are supported inside the chapter by the general narrative subject: the anticipation and the consumption of food. They are reinforced by the general structure of the book because the chapter in question, the eighth, is related as a Homeric parallel to the episode of "Lestrygonians." It is 1:00 p.m. and, as Stuart Gilbert tells us, the organ of the episode is the *oesophagus* and thus the technique is *paristaltic*. A few lines beneath those just quoted (still Joyce's example) Bloom looks at feminine silk garments in a window. Suddenly he is assaulted with oriental memories and sensual desires (the connection is made possible by the suggestions due to the reading of the name of an import company, Agendath Netaim). A blending of desire and memory with all the senses creates the enchantment of the moment and assumes the form of a physical appetite, which is transformed into a ravenous aspiration: "A warm human plumpness settled down on his brain. His brain yielded. Perfume of embraces all him assailed. With hungered flesh obscurely, he mutely craved to adore" (*U* 168).

Even here, an interplay of references inside the chapter and a system of references to the Homeric schema confirm the suggestions: the companions of Ulysses fall victim to Antiphates, king of the cannibal Lestrygonians because they are attracted, seduced as Joyce suggests, by the appearance of his daughter. In the Joycean text, the feminine motif enters as an element of seduction and resolves itself in a motif of gastronomy.

Inside the schema, Joyce uses every element of a seasoned modern poetics, with ample recourse to asyntactical arrangements which envelop the reader in a net of semantic suggestions without necessitating any single choice. It is still Joyce, referring to the quoted sentence "perfume of embraces all...," who calls to our attention the diverse ways in which this series of words could be organized. One finds a free play of the suggestive gamut by use of a technique that undoubtedly owes much to the syntax of the symbolists and, at the same time, to a rigid correspondence between phonetic and semantic suggestion. On the basis of this tension between order and syntactic liberty, the stimuli of the two quoted passages are enriched by other implications. Everything converges to reiterate the sensual characteristics of the petty bourgeois Bloom, to redesign the character for the thousandth time.

These two examples suffice to outline a general tendency, for the book is interwoven with devices of this type. Such are the onomatopoetics in "Sirens," in the formal parallels between the physio-psychological process in "Nausicaa" and the rhythm of the discourse describing it, which is rendered even more meaningful by the analogy — elementary as symbol but poetically effective — of the streaking rocket that explodes in the sky.

They are further displayed in the interlacing of ideas that evolves in each interior monologue; in the development of symbols of quasi-classical origin, such as the rod (scepter, rolled newspaper, baton of the blind tuner, ashplant of Stephen), or the key which appears over and over again in nearly obsessive form as a phallic symbol, recall to the homestead, sign of an attainable fatherland, clue to possible interpretations of various cyphers, symbol of power, etc.

In all of these cases, the system of suggestions does not go beyond the book to suggest a possible Absolute, a Verb as it was for Mallarmé. The multiple suggestions are systematically linked by internal relationships. It is true that there are many exits, that the same symbol can send us back simultaneously to the Trinitarian model, to the Homeric parallel, to the technical structure of the chapters, to the minor key symbols that strategically support the frame of the book without ever interjecting a definite rule as to how to interpret it. Nevertheless, the reader is always compelled to look for his interpretation within the book. The book is a labyrinthic territory where it is possible to move in many directions and to discover an infinite series of choices; but it is at the same time a closed universe, a cosmos beyond which there is nothing. Thus the scholastic Ordo closes the book in a net of *fidelia signacula* and, at the same time, establishes it as an *open* message.

Once again Joyce has succeeded and has reconciled two apparently opposed poetics. He has paradoxically superimposed the classical order onto the world of disorder which is accepted and recognized as the place of the contemporary artist. The resulting image of this universe bears a surprising affinity with that of contemporary culture. Edmund Wilson was perhaps the first to see and to realize the true nature of *Ulysses*:

> Joyce is indeed really the great poet of a new phase of the human consciousness. Like Proust's or Whitehead's or Einstein's world, Joyce's world is always changing as it is perceived by different observers and by them at different times. It is an organism made up of "events" which may be taken as infinitely inclusive or infinitely small and each of which involves all the others; and each of these events is unique. Such a world cannot be presented in terms of such artificial abstractions as have been conventional in the past: solid institutions, groups, individuals, which play the parts of distinct durable entities—or even of solid psychological factors: dualism of good and evil, mind and matter, flesh and spirit, instinct and reason; clear conflicts between passion and duty, between conscience and interest. Not that these conceptions are left out of Joyce's world: they are all there in the minds of the characters; and the realities they represent are there, too. But everything is reduced to terms of "events" like those of modern physics and philosophy—events which make up a "continuum," but which may be taken as infinitely small (Wilson, 1931, pp. 177-78).

The Metaphor of the New Science

Ulysses appears perfectly aligned with the world view of the new science, open in a provocative way, often with prophetic intuitions, to the issues of modern cultural anthropology, ethnology, and psychology. At the same time, it appears perfectly aligned with the contemporary arts, open to all the avant-gardes of our century. *Ulysses* has such richness of implication that it is possible to speak of its impressionism or its expressionism, to discuss its "cubist" approach, its cinematographic way of editing, its "variation of frequencies" that, in episodes like "Cyclops" with their alternation of comic deformation and mystical revelation, deliver "in their dissonance such an effect of intensity that makes one think about the music of Schoenberg or Alban Berg" (Cambon, 1963).[13]

Thus *Ulysses* appears as the incredible image of a world that supports itself, almost by miracle, on the preserved structures of an old world which are accepted for their formal reliability but denied in their substantial value. *Ulysses* represents a moment of transition for contemporary sensitivity. It appears as the drama of a dissociated consciousness that tries to reintegrate itself, finding, at the core of dissociation, a possible recovery by directing itself in opposition to its old frames of reference. In this sense the episode "Wandering Rocks" is exemplary. In its eighteen paragraphs the same episode is seen, and therefore measured, from eighteen points of view, in eighteen diverse spatial situations, and in eighteen distinct moments at different hours of the day. The procession of the viceroy which winds across Dublin thereby assumes eighteen aspects according to the space-time situation from which it is measured. This episode has been interpreted as an image of an Einsteinian universe. But if we examine each paragraph of the episode, we realize that the complexity of the space-time continuum rests upon narrative devices that are among the most comprehensible of the book, and if one did not consider the relativity model, the episode could be seen as one of the exercises of *ordo artificialis* studied by the medieval *artes rethoricae*. What we see here is the image of a new universe which survives because of the superimposition of Euclidean structures, a traditional geometry that provides the illusion of a renewed space. *Ulysses* appears a bit like an enormous treatise on quantum physics which paradoxically subdivides its material in the manner of the *Summa Theologiae* and freely uses concepts and examples from early Greek physics. It is thus a treatise in which one says "locus" and thinks of the electron as a wave of indeterminate position, or else, one says "energy quantum" and thinks of the Aristotelian *dynamis*.

Founded on such an ambiguous and precarious base, the book succeeds in being revelatory because the contradictions of its poetics are those of our culture.[14] However, if defined in terms of an implicit or explicit poetics, as the final effect of a series of operative proposals, *Ulysses* could not bear analysis. Once again, the Joycean poetics serve little for understanding Joyce and more for understanding the history of contemporary poetics. Joyce, with the explosive vigor of the artist who instinctively surpasses the apories of an uncertain philosophy, delivers a work that goes well beyond his poetics. It is for this that Joyce succeeds in sustaining two, three, four poetics. In the end, replete with a healthy mass of theoretical contradictions, *Ulysses* stands as a pure narrative work, as a story, as an epic tale, paradoxically surviving as an arrival point of the great romantic tradition, as the last "well-made" novel, as the last great theater in which human figures, historical events, and an entire society move in full action.

"Ulysses" as a *"Well-Made"* Novel

It has been observed that the symbolist poets, who yearned for *The Work*, the total Book, the metaphysical summary of a History without Time, failed in their task because they lacked the principal characteristic of Dante, Homer, or Goethe. These poets were able to create a total Book which united Heaven and Earth, Past and Present, History and Eternity because they turned their gaze towards the historical reality that circumscribed them. Only through this reality, that of the Greeks or of medieval Europe, did they succeed in giving form to an entire universe. The symbolists, on the contrary, having no interest in the world in which they lived, sought to attain the total Book in other ways, by erasing contemporary reality rather than penetrating it and by working on quotations rather than live experience.

With *Ulysses* we can speak of a great epic of the classical mode, like Dante's *Commedia*, conceived in Dublin rather than Florence. The book encompasses a grandiose mass of experience and the totality of the problems of contemporary man. In this respect the cultural reminiscences are overwhelmed by the vitality of the realistic, contemporary "presences" that crowd it.

Let us accept the conventions of the orders superimposed on the free proliferation of the *coup en largeur* and use them without thinking of the theoretical contradictions they carry. At this point, all the problems that await philosophical reflection disappear. We no longer ask whether individual personages exist in *Ulysses* or in the reality of a single consciousness. Gradually we forget any pre-established category because we are brought into the orbit of the "reality." Joyce gives us a new image of the man-world relationship and challenges the unresolved duality of the classical vision of the world. The young man Stephen still felt the anguish of dualism and tried to rediscover a possible unity through the enchanted moment of epiphany. But an epiphany, in order to realize a fictive unity of the world, dissolve its reality into an arbitrary act of imagination. On the contrary, in the new anthropology of *Ulysses*, any abstract distinction between soul and body, mind and matter, good and evil, idea and nature disappears.

Let us reread Bloom's philistine and "economic" monologues in which the presence of the city with its traffic, sounds, odors, and colors are grafted on to the evasions of fantasy, the pathetic needs of the soul and the desires of the flesh. Let us reread Molly's monologue in which a simple thermal sensation creates an explosion of the most elementary passions and the most profound female sentiments, the reasons of the flesh and maternity, the calls of the womb and the soul. Let us reread Stephen's monologues in which external facts are translated into abstract references, syllogistic games and metaphysical anguish; corporal stimuli become cultural quotations and erudite memories become sensomotor stimuli. At this point we witness the conversion of the ancient medieval Cosmos, theater of the struggle between the pure and impure, Heaven and Earth, into the undifferentiated, total horizon of the world. This world is ruled by an original ambiguity which existed before and lies beneath the distinctions later introduced by a science that must work by rigid categories. It is in the presence of the *Lebenswelt* before it vanishes into the shadows of reason, that our origin and nature, as discovered by contemporary phenomenology, must be sought. Against this presence operative and provisional distinctions—useful tools of organized knowledge which we have converted to idols out of laziness— crumble. Rational means are indispensable to cope with the world on rational terms. Yet, *they are not the world*.

In the moment in which the rhetorical order is grafted on to the disorder of the *coupe en largeur* and the two aspects melt together, permitting us to orient ourselves within the very heart of chaos, a type of order takes shape which is no longer a formal pattern but the very order of our "being-in-the-world," our "being-in-nature," our "to-be-nature." There is a page in the fourth chapter of *Ulysses*, disagreeable but essential, in which Bloom relieves himself while reading a fragment of a newspaper found in the jakes. This is not a simple "naturalistic" note. What is described here, contraction by contraction, is the complex game of peristaltic movement in which Bloom's body is involved. But the muscular rhythm is not autonomous. It runs parallel with the flow of thoughts inspired by the reading. The two orders of events are continuously interacting: the thoughts are directed by the muscular rhythm and these are stimulated or retarded by the stream of consciousness. In effect, there is no longer a flow of consciousness separated from the muscular rhythm. There is no longer a "primauté du spirituel" or a determinism of physical processes. The rhythm of Bloom banally seated in the water closet is truly a natural, integrated, and unified rhythm without univocal relations of cause and effect and thus without an *Ordo* to function as a hierarchy, a formal simplification of entities or events. Here we have a concrete field of interacting events in this sordid but real moment (and that which is real cannot be sordid in a universe in which the possibility for a necessary and stable set of priorities has collapsed). In this moment, compacted but exact, the *Weltanschauung* which dominates the entire book appears. It is the epic of the un-significant, of the *bêtise*, of the un-chosen, because the world is actually the total horizon of insignificant events which bind themselves in continuous constellations, each one the beginning and the end of a vital relation, center and periphery, first cause and last effect of a chain of meetings and oppositions, parenthoods, and contradictions. Good or bad, this is the world with which contemporary man must deal, be it through abstract science or concrete everyday experience. This is the world he is learning to accept, acknowledging it as his country of origin.

NOTES

[1] "Limits of the diaphane.... Limit of the diaphane in. Why in? Diaphane, adiaphane." Aristotle's text is *De Anima*, VII, 30 a.

[2] See Cambon (1953). Noon (1957, p. 113) remarks that there is an indirect reference to Berkeley in this shift from cosmos to chaos, "Who ever anywhere will read these writ-

Ulysses

ten words? Signs on a white field": the world as a message sent to men. The same chapter has a reference to the German terms "nacheinander" and "nebeneinander," in order to indicate temporal and spatial qualities of perceptions, the ineluctable modalities of the visible and of the audible. Paci (1962) suggests a reference to the phenomenology of Edmund Husserl, a philosopher who, to the best of our knowledge, Joyce did not know. It is not necessary, however, to look for direct influences: Joyce is approaching the modern philosophy of perception in its whole, thus echoing imprecise and indirect suggestions from secondhand readings. What is experienced here is a world perceived in its interaction with the human subject, without sharp distinction between *in* and *out*, mind and things.

[3] See Litz (1961, ch. 2). Contemporary aesthetics and literary criticism has insisted on technics as a way of "giving shape" which concerns not only so-called "form" but also the content of a text. As for the passage from the "lump of experience" to the "achieved content" see Scherer (1948); Eliot (1932) says that art imposes a rhythm to the order of action. Frank (1964) analyzes the way in which the organization of narrative materials creates a "spatial form" in Flaubert, Proust and Joyce.

[4] Quoted in Edel (1955), ch. 1.

[5] There is a difference between the point of view of the psychologist and the novelist. To William James, the stream of consciousness was the guarantee of the existence of a personal subject: when analyzing one's own stream of consciousness, one becomes aware of the difference between internal and external experiences. But when the novelist registers events of a human conscience and events of the external words *on the page*, at the same time, by means of the same stylistic formulas, any difference between internal and external vanishes and the reader receives only the impression of an undifferentiated, "behavioristic" description. The problem of the "materialization" of the imagined image and its autonomy from external reality has been one of the most dramatic issues of traditional psychology; see J.P. Sartre, *L'imagination* (Paris, 1936).

[6] Cf. Gilbert (1930), Tindall (1950), Gorman (1940), Budgen (1934), Noon (1957), Empson (1956)

[7] In Honorius, *Liber duodecim questionum* (*Patrologia Latina* 170, col. 1179) one finds an interesting definition of the mutual implications of all things which could be taken as a witty synopsis of *Ulysses*: "Similiter corporalia vocum discrimina imitantur, dum in varia genera, in varias species, in individua, in formas, in numero separantur; quae omnia concorditer consonant, dum legem sibi insitam quasi tinnulis modis servant. Reciprocum sonum reddunt spiritum et corpus, angelus et diabolus, coelum et infernum, ignis et aqua, aer et terra, dulce et amarum, molle et durum, et sic coetera in hunc modum."

[8] See E. Faral, *Les art poétiques du XIIme et du XIIIme siècle* (Paris: Champion, 1923), p. 60.

[9] All of these references to medieval tradition could seem a mere erudite *divertissement*; however, it is Joyce himself who says that his roots must be found *there*. See in *CW* (p. 27) the juvenile essay "The Study of Languages" (1898), which reveals the influences of the medieval rhetorical tradition in the University College—where style, syntax, and rhetoric are defined "the champions and the exponents, in what way soever, of Truth."

[10] If Joyce had had a direct knowledge of the text of Aquinas, one could say that it was not by chance that he gave so much importance to the Trinitarian problem. As a matter of fact, the pages on the three criteria of Beauty appear in the *quaestio*, dealing

with the names of the three Persons of the Trinity (*Summa Th.*, I, 39, 8 co).

[11] Oh the relationship between this Trinitarian schema and Sabellian heresy, see Noon (1957, pp. 94 ff.); Kaye (1959), on the contrary, judges the Joycean schema an orthodox one. The Sabellian heresy identifies the Father and the Son in such a way that no mediation on the part of the Holy Ghost is required. If one recognizes the orthodoxy of the Stephen-Son and Bloom-Father relationship, then one is obliged to identify Molly as the mediating element. Thus, to avoid a charge of blasphemy, one should charge Joyce with heresy.

[12] Pound (1922), on the contrary, interprets this interplay of correspondences as a medieval residue, mere scaffolding.

[13] On Joyce and relativity theory, see Broch (1936). On Joyce and cultural anthropology, see Tindall (1950), Cambon (1953). Cf. also Joyce, letter to L. Gillet, September 8, 1938, for the discovery of Bérard on the Phoenician origins of the *Odyssey*. For the parallelisms between Joyce and Schoenberg, cf. particularly Schoenberg, "Composition with Twelve Notes," in *Style and Idea* (New York: Philosophical Library, 1950).

[14] *Ulysses* reproposes the opposition, typical of contemporary science, between the causal determinism of Einsteinian physics and the indeterminacy and probabilism advocated by quantum mechanics. Joyce tries to reduce and harmonize such a discrepancy. It is worth noting that many contemporary scientific discussions deal with such projects; see, for instance, Werner Heisenberg. The author of the uncertainty principle speaks of a possible Pythagorean and Platonic mathematical harmony of the universe: "in modern quantum theory there can be no doubt that the elementary particles will finally also be mathematical forms. . . . Therefore, the mathematical forms that represent the elementary particles will be solutions of some eternal laws of motion for matter. . . . Some statements of ancient philosophy are rather near to those of modern science. This simply shows how far one can get by combining the ordinary experience of nature that we have without doing experiments with the untiring effort to get some logical order into this experience to understand it from general principles" (*Physics and Philosophy* [London: Allen and Unwin, 1958], pp. 68-70). Thus Heisenberg, in his late writings, looks for stable criteria of order and explicitly for the rediscovery of some "Logos." In Joyce, however, this quest and the attempt to reconcile classical order with a polyvalent universe is limited to the project of *Ulysses*. As seen in the third chapter, *Finnegans Wake* offers a different solution.

III. Finnegans Wake

Scriptorum tanta barbarie est, et tantis vitiis spurcissimis sermo confusus ut nec qui loquatur nec quibus argumentis velit probare quod loquitur, potuerim intelligere. Totum enim tumet, totum iacet: attollit per se singula, et quasi debilitatus coluber, in ipso conatu frangitur. Non est contentus nostro, id est, humano more, loqui, altius quidam egreditur. . . . Praeterea sic involvit omnia et quibusdam inextricabilus nodis universa perturbat, ut illo plautinarum litterarum ei possit adaptari: "Has quidem praeter Sybillam leget memo." Quae sunt haec portenta verborum? . . . Totum incipit, totum pendet ex altero: nescias quid cohaereat. . . et reliquus sermo omni materiae convenit. . . .

— St. Jerome, *Adversus Jovinianum* 1

It may seem that *Ulysses* violates the techniques of the novel beyond all limit, but *Finnegans Wake* passes even this limit. It may seem that *Ulysses* demonstrates all the possibilities of language, but *Finnegans Wake* takes language beyond any boundary of communicability. It may seem that *Ulysses* represents the most arduous attempt to give physiognomy to chaos, but *Finnegans Wake* defines itself as *Chaosmos* and *Microchasm* and constitutes the most terrifying document of formal instability and semantic ambiguity that we possess.

What project was Joyce pursuing in beginning this work seventeen years before giving it definitively to print? The answer is complex if one follows the mass of proposals, critical observations and explanations that the author gives of his *Work in Progress* in the various letters and oral declarations from 1923 to 1939.[1] A search for the poetics of the *Wake*, a poetics understood as a system of operative rules that preside in making the work, becomes a desperate task because the various drafts show that these rules change as the work progresses and that the final design is very different from the first one. The book, as we shall see, is the continuous poetics of itself, and an examination of the work from any of its parts will help us clarify the ideas upon which it is based.

According to the early project, since *Ulysses* is the story of a day, *Finnegans Wake* will be the story of a night. Thus, from the very beginning the idea of sleep and dream presides over the general design of the work which arranges itself, Joyce notes, a piece at a time like a mah jong puzzle:

> In writing of the night I really could not, I felt I could not, use words in their ordinary connections. Used that way, they do not express how things are in the night, in the different stages — conscious, then semi-conscious, then unconscious. I found that it could not be done with words in their ordinary relations and connections. When morning comes, of course, everything will be clear again (Eastman, 1931).

Joyce lived in Zurich, in the very years in which Freud and Jung were publishing some of their principal works. While he showed no interest in the fathers of psychoanalysis, Ellmann speaks of his deep sensitivity for oneiric experience. The *Wake* must have been constructed according to the logic of a dream, where the identities of people are confused and exchanged, and a single idea, or the memory of a single fact, takes shape in a series of strangely connected symbols. The same thing happens to the words, which are merged in the most free and unexpected way, in order to suggest a series of disparate ideas with a single expression. This too is oneiric logic, but it is also a linguistic technique whose use has illustrious precedents. The Church was founded on a calembour, Joyce recalls ("Tu es Petrus, etc. . . ."), and such an example constitutes sufficient authorization. From the beginning, *Finnegans Wake* announces what it will be — a nocturnal epic of ambiguity and metamorphoses, the myth of a death and a universal rebirth in which each figure and each work will stand in place of all the others. It will be an epic without clear divisions between the events, so that each event may implicate the others to form an elementary unity that does not exclude the collision and opposition between contraries.

The Poetics of Vico's Cycles

Having determined what Joyce wished to do, we must now ask why he proposed this task. What did the project of the new work offer him after *Ulysses*? Since *Ulysses* is an example of a paradoxical equilibrium among the forms of a rejected world and the disordered substance of the new, then the successive work will strive to be a representation of the chaos and the multiplicity within which the author seeks the most congenial models of order. The cultural experience that inspired this decision was the reading of Vico.

We say "reading" and not "acceptance." As Joyce has explicitly affirmed, he did not find in Vico a philosophy in which "to believe" but an author who stimulated his imagination and opened new horizons. Upon finishing *Ulysses*, Joyce had succeeded in collecting the vivacity of lived experience but was forced to imprison it in the net of a foreign cultural order. In Vico he discovered new issues. Joyce already knew Vico, but when considering the new project, he felt the need to read his words more attentively, particularly *La Scienza Nuova*. In 1926 Joyce writes that he would like to draw selectively upon the theories of Vico, using them only insofar as they are useful to him. But these theories became increasingly important in his eyes and serve to mark various phases of his life (*L* 241). Joyce could not avoid associating Viconian teachings with ideas assimilated from contemporary philosophy and science. In a letter dated 1927 (*L* 249) a rather obscure reference appears in which the name of Vico is associated not only with Croce, which would be natural, but Einstein.

It is understandable that Joyce was struck primarily by Vico's need for a world order not to be sought outside events, as in *Ulysses*, but within these very events, within the heart of a history that was envisioned as alternating *corsi* and *ricorsi*. Joyce freely associates this theory with oriental conceptions of the circularity of Being. Thus, in the fabric of the *Wake*, the historicist theory of *ricorsi* becomes an esoteric notion of an "eternal return" in which the historical aspect of development is overlaid by the circular identity of everything and the continuous reproposing of original archetypes. The assimilation of oriental concepts into a Viconian philosophy reveals the syncretism typical of Joyce's ideological choices. Joyce, in fact, has said that the Neapolitan philosopher helped to stimulate his own fantasy rather than to discover any "science."

Vico was also useful by providing Joyce with a developmental schema for his Brunian and Cusanian convictions, a model in which he might locate the movement of oppositions within a dynamic framework. Vico must also have impressed Joyce by the enthusiasm with which he stressed the importance of myth and language, his vision of a primitive society which creates, by linguistic "tropes," its own image of the world. Joyce was undoubtedly struck by Vico's image of those "few giants" (and Finn MacCool was a giant) who notice for the first time the divine voice through the thunder ("quando il cielo finalmente folgorò, tuonò con folgori et tuoni spaventosissimi," Book 11) and feel the need to name the unknown. When the thunder of *Scienza Nuova* appears in the first page of *Finnegans Wake*, it has been translated into a sort of "gestural" and mimetic language. This language is primitive and barbaric because it is basically onomatopoeic. At the same time, it is overloaded with culture because it is built upon the linguistic fragments of previous languages by juxtaposing different foreign synonyms of the word "thunder": "bababadalgharaghtakamminarronnkonnbronntonnerronntuonnthunntrovarrhounawnskawntoohoohoordenenthurnuk!"

Joyce must have derived from Vico the need for a "mental language common to all nations," interpreting it in a personal way within the polyglotism of the *Wake*. Joyce also learned the value of the philological sciences which discover, through language, the property and the origin of things "according to the order of ideas by which the history of language must proceed."[3] He also assimilated the foundation and philological interpretation of myth and comparative languages. In addition, he learned to collect "the great pieces of antiquity." Joyce accomplishes all these things at the level of language, in his own way.

Joyce also drew upon Vico's justification of a primitive poetic logic in which one speaks according to "un parlare fantastico per sostanze animate," a poetic logic based on the *primi tropi*, the elementary tropes, the basic rhetorical figures. Among those "the brightest is the metaphor, and because it is the brightest, it is the most necessary and complex and is ever praised for it confers sense and passion upon meaningless things" (*Scienza Nuova*, II).

Also from Vico is the idea that fallen man, having lost any hope of being helped by Nature, looks to a superior thing for salvation. Joyce, with his taste for compromise, couples this Viconian striving for salvation with the Brunian idea of the discovery of a god within the unity of the world and not beyond it. With these elements Joyce designs an image of the earthly cycle, with its *corsi* and *ricorsi*, that achieves salvation through the acceptance of the circularity through which it infinitely unfolds. Challenged by Vico's pages on the creativity of language, Joyce assimilates nature to culture and identifies what exists with what is said, the given of nature with the product of culture (the *verum* with the *factum*), and thereby conceives of the world as a dialectic of tropes. Only by individuating them, as in *Ulysses*, does Joyce confer a "sense and passion" upon "meaningless things."

The Poetics of the Pun

The "cultural" rationale of *Finnegans Wake* now becomes clear. Joyce has reduced reality to the world of myths, traditions, ancient fragments, the words by which man has designated his experiences. He has tried to meld these into the amalgam of the dream in order to find, in this original liberty, in this zone of fertile ambiguity, a new order of the universe delivered from the tyranny of the old traditions. The initial fall has established a cultivated state of barbarity, a primitive, uncivilized language built from the linguistic debris of many civilizations. Here everything moves in a primordial and disordered flow; everything is its own opposite; everything can collegate itself to all the others. No event is new for something similar has already happened; a *ricorso*, a connection, is always possible. If history is a continuous cycle of alternations and recurrences, then it does not have the characteristic of irreversibility that we are accustomed to confer upon it today. Rather, each event is simultaneous; past, present and future coincide. But since each thing exists to the extent that it is named, this whole movement, this game of continuous metamorphoses can only happen in words, and the pun, the calembour, is the mainspring of this process.

The pun is a figure ignored by classical rhetoric. Let us define it as a sort of pseudo-paronomasia which constitutes a forced embedding of two or more similar words. *Sang + sans + glorians + sanglot + riant* give "sansglorians." The pun is a continuity produced by reciprocal elisions so that one word can stand for another word, even if no word appears in its entirety.

According to the classical explanation, a metaphor entails the substitution of one word by another, the substituting word being the "vehicle" and the substituted word the "tenor." I can say "stars" instead of "eyes" or vice versa. With the pun, the inner mechanism changes: vehicle and tenor are simultaneously present, both embedded, reciprocally sending back one to another. In "Jungfraud's Messonge book" (FW 460) we detect, contemporaneously, *Jung +*

Freud + *young* + *fraud* + *Jungfrau* + *message* + *songe* + *mensonge*.
Sometimes, by a sort of *total* paronomasia, a given word wholly coin-
cides with the word it contains: this is the case of the "commodius
vicus of recirculation" which should bring back to Howth Castle and
Environs (*FW* 4). In Latin, a "vicus" is a path, and at the same time, it is
the Latin translation of "Vico." Thus the theory of Vico is taken as the
metaphor of a commodius "path" for interpreting events, and contemporaneously, a "path" is taken as the metaphor of Vico's thought.
Both the path and Vico's theory are "commodius," but the term (once
again a Latin one) paronomastically contains "Commodus," and the
refernce to an Emperor of the *empire à la fin de la décadence* refers
back to the syncretic approach of the book itself.

Obviously, the reader cannot pursue all of the references in the
course of a single reading. One is compelled to choose among possible interpretive paths and to disambiguate various levels of sense.
Contemporary semantics speaks of different "isotopies" of sense. The
decision to take "Vico" for "vicus" (or, vice versa, "vicus" for "Vico")
entails a totally different level of meaning. But even while moving at a
given level, one must be alert to the existence of the others which appear in the background, disturbing the linearity of the first and
stimulating the reader to feel an "uneasiness" and to suspect a "felic-
ity," a baroque "wit." In other words, one is compelled to find an
order and, at the same time, to realize that there are many possible
orders; a given choice does not eliminate the alternatives.

Finnegans Wake is an open work. For this reason it is a *scherzarade*
(game, charade, tale of Sheherazade), *vicocyclometer, collideoscope,
proteiform graph, polyhedron of scripture, meanderthale* and, finally,
a *work of doublecrossing twofold truths and devising tail-words*.

The most complete definition of this work can be found in the
series of definitions given of the famous illegible letter. It can be read
in many ways, like the book and the universe of which both the book
and the letter are the substitute. "Every person, place and thing in the
chaosmos of Alle anyway connected with the gobblydumped turkery
was moving and changing every part of the time," and in this "steady-
monologuy of the interiors" one finds "the Ostrogothic kakography
affected for certain phrases of Etruscan stabletalk and, in short, the
learning betrayed at almost every line's end"; because it is an "utterly
unexpected sinistrogyric return to one peculiar sore point in the past
...with some half-halted suggestion...indicating that the words
which follow may be taken in any order desired...unconnected,

principal, medial or final . . .," with the "lubricitous conjugation of the last with the first," we can find "a word as cunningly hidden in its maze of confused drapery as a fieldmouse in a nest of coloured ribbons." Once again, the work can be defined as a "prepronominal funferal, engraved and retouched and edgewiped and puddenpadded, very like a whale's egg farced with pemmican, as were it sentenced to be nuzzled over a full trillion times for ever and a night till his noodle sink or swim by that ideal reader suffering from an ideal insomnia" (*FW* 118-21).

Although Joyce has followed a rather arbitrary order of aggregation in composing these quotations, the book is made to support and request this operation. An infinity of allusions, contained in a word or resulting from the coupling of two words, escape the reader. Many of the allusions, in fact, escape the author himself, who has prepared a machinery of suggestion which, like any complex machine, is capable of operating beyond the original intentions of its builder. It is not necessary that the reader understand the exact meaning of every word and phrase; the force of the text resides in its permanent ambiguity and in the continuous resounding of numerous meanings which seem to permit selection but in fact eliminate nothing.

In order to obtain such a "cybernetic" result, the freedom of the reader's choices must be "directed" by the text itself. To create the impression of a total lack of structure, a work of art must possess a strong underlying structure. The possibility of switching from one level to another could be effected only by a cunningly organized network of mutual relationships. This is the structural problem of the so-called contemporary "open works of art," in which the free interplay of ambiguities always presumes a *rule of ambiguation*.

If *Finnegans Wake* reflects the structure of the world through natural language, then it embodies the structure of natural language. Formal logic has suggested that natural languages have no logic. In fact, they are not ruled by a formal logic but by a rhetoric, a logic of substitutions. These are based upon an unexpressed "golden rule": everything can be substituted for everything else, provided there is an underlying network of possible connections established by a previous cultural convention. The operation of such a mechanism in *Finnegans Wake* could be clarified only by contemporary structural semantics, which is engaged in discovering and organizing the so-called "fields" of meaning into a sort of kinship system. For such a task, *Finnegans Wake* is a paramount laboratory model. Let us, for the time being, limit ourselves to a preliminary probing and assume that a word is a signifier conveying a signified or meaning. The lexemes offered by a dictionary are signifiers which are associated with certain signifieds by definitions, synonyms, and paraphrases. These signifieds are the culturally defined units that a given culture has recognized and organized into a system of relationships. Traditional rhetoric defines metaphors, for instance, as the substitution of a given signifier with another because of a similarity between their signifieds or part of their signifieds. Thus a strong man can be designated with the signifier "bull" if a cultural convention has established that both the bull and the man are characterized (as the definitional composition of their meanings) by the element "force." Other rhetorical figures, for instance paronomasia, associate two words because of an existing similarity between signifiers irrespective of their etymology. "Sleep" can become the paronomastic counterpart of "slip" because of a phonic similarity which suggests a meaning-parenthood that the vocabulary did not foresee.

Puns are built on the basis of this second procedure: "sleep" plus "slip" gives "slipping" (beauty). Because the similarity between the signifiers of the two words has been physically reinforced by a *lexical merging*, various hidden semantic affinities can emerge. When one has shown a phonic affinity between "Sheherazade," "charade" and the Italian word "scherzo" (joke, trick), the resulting pun "Scherzarade" is more than a mere *forced paronomasia*. It is, at this point, an elliptical discourse: the tale of Sheherazade is viewed as an enigmatic joke and the book, of which the pun is one of its definitions, is presented as an unending discourse, proceeding through enigmas and taking a series of verbal tricks as its surface form. At this point, one is entitled to choose one's own level of reading and to understand the book as a fairy tale, a puzzle, a mere joke, and so on. In contrast, there are cases in which the semantic affinity between two items induces the author to produce an affinity between signifiers through the insertion of a third word. There is no phonic similarity between the vehicles "Freud" and "Jung," but there is a cultural parenthood between the theories of the two authors. Thus, the authors become the metonymical substitute for their own theories and vice versa. These similarities are organized by our culture into the same semantic field — one concerning the study of dreams. Once the cultural parenthood between Freud and Jung is detected, Joyce looks for a possible phonic link and finds the German word "jungfrau," into which Freud and Jung can be embedded as "jungfraud." In order to render the phonic merging more phonetically similar to "jungfrau," "Freud" must be transformed into "fraud." (It is only a reconstructive hypothesis that this third result depends upon the previous operation, for Joyce could have proceeded in the opposite way. But since we are not trying to analyze the mental processes of the author but the linguistic structure of the text, we can approach the pun "jungfraud" from any direction.) As a final result, we face a word which imposes upon us the recognition of a similarity between psychoanalysis, oneiric processes, youth, fraud, virgin. Since this pun is contextually associated with "messonge," message + songe + mensonge (message + dream + lie), the potential short circuit between the two puns "Jungfraud" and "messonge" suggests a cluster of ideas concerning various relationships between the theory of dreams, sex, messages sent by the unconscious, the capacity of these messages to lie through a disguising virginal naiveté, etc.

In order to build the pun, an underlying network of cultural associations must exist. To isolate such a network, one can penetrate the field through any of its verbal accesses, not only through those that compose the pun but also through those words that compose other contextually surrounding *calembours*. Let us try to reach "jungfraud" through another of the *mot-valises* appearing in the book, for instance "meandertale." Paronomastically speaking, "meandertale" suggests "Neanderthal," a word which does not exist as such in *Finnegans Wake*. The lexeme "Neanderthal" generates, by phonic similarity, "meander," "tal" (in German, "valley"), "tale." By their merging, one gets the puns "meandertale" and "meanderthalltale" (*FW* 18-19).

The table on page 71 reveals that any of the elementary lexemes composing the pun could generate various paths of association, by phonic or semantic affinity. In other words, by laws of phonetic and semantic similarity, each lexeme can become the "patriarch" of a series of associations, each of these composed by a list of lexemes, each of which can become, in turn, the patriarch of other associative chains.

Thus, the book is a labyrinth of "coloured ribbons" in which space and time are confusedly woven into a flowering maze of cyclical connections. These lead through the paths of dream to the archetypal offspring of the primordial myths and, at the same time, through a culturalized landscape where the modern disciplines of the unconscious reveal the inner mechanism of our "internal fabric." There we find the mechanism of the Id and the mechanism of the Tale, both made of lapsuses, sudden revelations, lies and frauds, *trompe-l'oeils* and leading clues, ambiguities and an abundance of interpretations. Many paths and many issues lead into the circular nest in which no issue exists, since every issue brings the reader, by a "commodius vicus of recirculation," back to the HCE.

The field that we have outlined utilizes only a restricted quantity of the lexemes existing in *Finnegans Wake*. While it would be interesting to trace the entire system of interconnections, such a task would require one to reduce the work, a layer at a time, to each of its possible readings. Every lexeme in every reading might then become the patriarch of a new chain of associations, sending back to other fields, so that by connecting the fields together, one could trace an unending ribbon of associations. Every word of the book becomes the main issue that introduces every other word, a sort of topological maze in which everything is both the deep "inside" and the peripheral "outside." For another clue to the book, consider the Cusanian category of *coincidentia oppositorum*.

The Coincidentia Oppositorum

In the chapter in which Shaun the postman pleads against Shem the penman, Joyce recounts the fable of *The Ondt and the Gracehoper* (*The Ant and the Grasshopper*). Shaun identifies with the thrifty ant and denounces in Shem the thoughtlessness of the grasshopper. But in the heart of Shaun's pejoration, Joyce extols the "Gracehoper," the artist turned towards the future, towards growth and development. Shem is thus symbolized by the tree and the traditionalist immobility of the ant is symbolized by the stone, "ant" being deformed into "ondt" which signifies "evil" in Danish.

The Gracehoper passes the whole day singing ballads like those of Tim Finnegan (to thus compose *Finnegans Wake*): "For if sciencium . . . can mute uns nought, 'a thought, abought the Great Sommbboddy within the Omniboss, perhops an artsaccord . . . might sings ums tumtin abutt the Little Newbuddies that ring his panch" (*FW* 414). For this reason, the grasshopper sings, "hoppy . . . of his joyicity." But the ant is serious. He is a perfect chairman and is opposed to adventure in time, claiming the primacy, the solidity, and the inalterability of space. The ant questions why the grasshopper conducts a life of dissi-

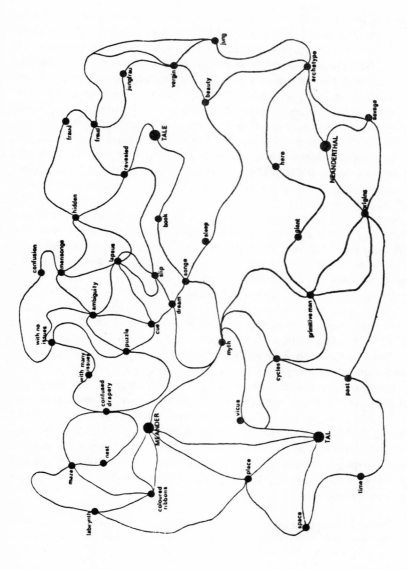

Reproduced by U. Eco, *Le forme del contenuto*
(Milano: Bompiani, 1971), p. 105.

pation and debt. The ant is a "conformed aceticist and aristotaller" and alluding to him, Joyce speaks of "aquinatance." The grasshopper and the ant are "umsummables," the dialectic between the tree and the rock no longer enters into the possible *summa* of an Aristotelian philosophy. That of the grasshopper is a "veripatetic imago of the impossible . . . actually and presumptuably sinctifying chronic's despair" (*FW* 417). His chronic desperation is due to his wandering in time, *chronos*, in accepting the flow of history and sin against the strength of the rock, the solidity of space. Nonetheless, there is no definitive choice between the ideal of the ant and that of the grasshopper. These are "umsummables" but complementary. The dialectic of order and adventure puts order into a crisis but defines the very condition of adventure.

In order to give philosophical stature to the poetics of the *Wake*, we shall refer once again to those definitions of cosmic reality given by Nichola da Cusa and Giordano Bruno.[2] *Finnegans Wake* is the work in which Nichola's *coincidentia oppositorum* meets Bruno's identity of contraries, ". . . by the coincidance of their contraries reamalgamerge in that identity of undiscernibles" (*FW* 49-50). (The "identity of undiscernibles," Leibniz' phrase, is a category of logic philosophically irreconcilable with the coincidence of the contraries, reminding us of Joyce's fascination with the pure "music of ideas" and producing a rhetorical oxymoron.) In this wave of totality in which negations and antipathies are polarized ("equals of opposites . . . and polarised for reunion by the symphysis of their antipathies . . ."), nothing is drawn up that does not continually resurface. As Bruno conceives, there is an "internal sense" of each body such that each finite, limited being participates in the life of everything without losing its individuality. Each is attracted and repelled by other bodies because of sympathy and antipathy. No other poetic norm could have been more fully adopted by Joyce in his last works than this Brunian recommendation:

> You will discover that you have truly reached this level of progress when you are able to achieve a clear unity, beginning from a confused plurality . . . beginning from multiple, formless parts, to adapt to oneself the whole that has received form and unity (*Libri physicorum Aristotelis explanati*, Op. Lat. III).

Finnegans Wake accomplishes this dictate by being the poetics of itself. It is not possible to clarify the meaning of a single term and its relationship with all the others if one does not attend to the total network of meanings. Each word serves to clarify the sense of the book; each is a perspective about the book and gives a sense and direction to one of its possible readings. At the aesthetic level, this operation actualizes the Cusanian doctrine of the *complicatio*: in each thing is realized everything and everything is in each thing. Each thing finally appears as a perspective on the universe and a microcosmic model of it. Although everything is the reduction of the whole, no thing can be equal to another, for each conserves an irreducible singularity that permits it to reflect the cosmos in an unexpected and individual manner.[3] It is not by chance that Joyce cites Nichola da Cusa several times, because it is actually in this author, in the crucial historical knot in which scholasticism dissolves, that a humanistic-modern sensibility is born. In Nichola, Joyce finds a vision of a polydimensional reality, the infinite possible perspectives of a universal form that can be seen under different visual angles, in endless and complementary profiles.

This new sensibility is still imbued with medieval reminiscence, with the cabalistic and magical sensibilities of Bruno's Renaissance. Although it is still far from the modern world view, this new perspective signals the rupture of the medieval faith in the inalterability and identity of forms. Joyce uses the references to Nichola to destroy his youthful Thomist aesthetic. For St. Thomas, a form is a tetragonal, univocal, compact component of a universe made of individual, discernible forms. These forms can have a disposition (*appetitus*) to become another form, but this disposition does not affect their individual nature. In Nichola da Cusa, these foundations are trembling and the cosmos breaks apart in the faceting of a thousand possibilities. The finite world of the Middle Ages becomes, as it will be with Bruno, the infinity of possible worlds. The Brunian universe is animated by an incessant tendency towards transformation. Each finite individual, in its tendency towards the infinite, moves towards ulterior formations. The dialectic of the finite and infinite is accomplished only in the ceaseless process of cosmic metamorphosis. Each being has in itself the seed of future forms that guarantee its infinity.[4] Joyce had read Bruno's *De l'Infinito Universo e Mondi*,[5] and one of the most implicit and explicit axioms of the *Wake* is that of the infinity of worlds, unified by the metamorphic nature of each word, the willingness of each etymon to immediately become something else and explode in new semantic directions. Just as Bruno arrived at this vision of the world as a result of the discovery of Copernicus (and saw in it the fall of a static and limited conception of the Cosmos), so the young Joyce, through Bruno, discovered the way to cast the stable and circumscribed universe of scholasticism into doubt.[6]

Once again we find in Joyce the confluence between diverse poetics and discordant cultural suggestions. The last Joycean work fuses the Cusanian and Brunian image of the universe, the dictates of the late Romantic poetics, the universe of Baudelarian *correspondences* and Rimbaudian equivalences, Wagner's technique of leitmotiv and his program for a fusion of sound, word, and action. These symbolist suggestions come from Joyce's early readings and from the revelations of Symons's book. Together they translate, in another cultural context and upon more uncertain metaphysical ground, that cosmic music of the great Renaissance masters that awakens Stephen from his dogmatic slumber.

The Epiphany as an Epistemological Metaphor

In this Renaissance and late Romantic universe, however, phenomena exist that neither Bruno nor the symbolists could have foreseen. Like *Ulysses*, *Finnegans Wake* transposes, in the structure of its discourse, the phenomena described by contemporary science. The work thus becomes a grandiose *epistemological metaphor*. It is a metaphor—not a literal model but an analogy. Rather, it is a field of analogies, for *Finnegans Wake* does not embody one particular description of the world but utilizes contradictory images from diverse frameworks. It is as if the author has sensed new ways of seeing things and mirrored these different points of view, simultaneously, in his linguistic structures. Thus, in language, Joyce finds the possibility for a range of coexisting perspectives which, at the level of rigorous scientific conceptualization, would be mutually exclusive.

Finnegans Wake, for example, produces a crisis in the notions of time, identity and causal connections that suggests certain cosmological hypotheses that go beyond the theory of relativity itself. Consider a causal chain in which, given events A and B, it is established that B is born from A and that there is a line of succession from A to B that is established according to a temporal order. This type of causal chain has been defined as "open," in the sense that we move forward and are never able to return to the starting point. (When the scientist speaks of the "open" causal chain he uses the term in a very different sense than we have in speaking about the "Open Work" – Eco 1962, 1979.) An open causal chain actually represents the guarantee of a closed order of events in which connections proceed according to an irreversible order. But if a "closed" chain is established, then an event can become the cause of its own remote cause. In such a case it is no longer possible to attribute an order to time. This fact jeopardizes the principle of identity that provides the very possibility of establishing the difference between two events. In a closed causal chain, Reichenbach explains, it could happen that I meet the myself of ten years ago and converse with him and that ten years later, the same situation would be inevitably repeated, although my age would change. While the first time I was my younger self, the second time I would be the older one that converses with a third self and seeks to convince him that we are the same person or vice versa. This situation does not correspond to the physical universe in which we live. Nonetheless, in logical terms a universe of this type is thinkable and "formally," the "idea has no contradictions."[7]

Transposing the question to the level of narrative relations, we note that the traditional novel posited open causal chains in which an event A, the shipwreck of Robinson Crusoe for example, is to be seen as the irreversible cause of an ordered series of events B, C, D – life on the island, the meeting with Friday, the return to his country. It is not possible to reverse the causative chain and attribute Robinson's shipwreck to the fact that he would one day meet Friday.

In a book such as *Finnegans Wake*, however, the causal relationship of events is entirely different. The manner in which we understand a term totally changes the way in which we understand the term in the preceding pages, and the way in which we interpret an allusion deforms the very identity of its remote antecedents. It is not the case that the book finishes because it has begun in a certain way; rather, *Finnegans Wake* begins because it finishes in that way. In many science fiction stories time is reversible, permitting a contemporary character to meet Homer, Cromwell, or George Washington. In these cases, the reversibility of time is one fact among the contents of the story. In order to "speak about" this fact which defies the causal conception of time, the story semantically and syntactically respects all the linguistic causal relationships. By contrast, *Finnegans Wake* does not "speak" about temporal subversion; it speaks *by means of* causal subversion at the level of the "telling process," not that of the "told content." In the *Wake*, the co-presence of diverse historical identities arises because there exist precise structural and semantic conditions that deny the causal order to which we are accustomed. Semantically "closed" chains are established and, as a result, the total work permits the reader to freely construe the semantic universe according to a reversible order of causality.

The logic of causality is only one possible epistemological key. Consequently, we recognize in the *Wake*, even more than in *Ulysses*, a universe of relativity in which each word becomes "a space-time event,"[8] whose relations with other events change according to the position of the observer and the decisions that the observer makes when semantically provoked by each term. The *Wake* is thus a universe dominated by "isotropy," in the sense that in an appropriate system of coordinates, no single coordinate appears privileged to an observer looking in different directions. In such a system the universe appears identical in all directions and therefore isotropic. This universe is also "homogenous" in the following respect: given observers posted at different points in the universe who describe its history through diverse but suitably chosen systems of coordinates, the contents of these histories will be identical, making it impossible to distinguish one place from another.[9]

The *Wake* seems to verify this cosmological hypothesis, for its various interpretive keys establish directions of reading. But even here we must not look for the transposition of a single science. Joyce's statements about his use of *La Scienza Nuova* should make us cautious. In *Finnegans Wake* we witness only the imaginative counterthrusts of cultural facts: we do not have a translation but a paraphrase. Since it is not the paraphrase of one conceptual system alone but of many disconnected and often mutually contradictory systems, its suggestions cannot be synthesized into a unitary cultural model. The verification of diverse influences and connections does not provide the reader with a schematic framework in which to isolate a system of correspondences point by point. This material cannot be reduced to a systematic unity but only suggested by a dizzy explosion of the linguistic material. This constitutes the common ground of all contemporary culture – the experience of a new and changing image of the world, one which throws imagination and intelligence, sense and reason, fancy and logic into discord. In this context, the *Wake* is a work of mediation which shows that the new logic can find a corresponding image. But since no image can be translated into the abstract and univocal form of a proposition, the result of this operation is a series of ambiguous statements, rather, a series of "speech acts." If these images say anything, it is that the things which they suggest cannot be univocally defined. The *Wake* cannot "translate" the sense of vertigo produced by the new scientific and rational explanations of the world but can only "embody it." Thus the *Wake* becomes the linguistic image of the vertigo, a "whorled without aimed." This is its own way to render a new world, representable if not explicable.

The work provides a glimpse of this new form, but it does not try to define it. As Samuel Beckett suggests, *Finnegans Wake* does not deal with something, but it itself *is something* (Beckett, 1929). It is thus an "impersonal" construction that becomes the "objective correlative" of a personal experience. Were Joyce to describe this, he might say something like the following: the form of the universe has changed in an incomprehensible way; I have felt that our millenary interpretive criteria no longer work, and thus I give to you a substitute of our world, an endless world and a meaningless whirl. At least this substitute is a human product, posited, not given, founded on the cultural order of language as opposed to the order of nature. As such, since Vico said *"verum ipsum factum,"* we can understand and accept it.

What is the relationship between this world and the real world? Once again, the poetics of the epiphany can aid us. From a context of events the poet has isolated what was meaningful to him (this time the universe of linguistic relations) and has offered us what he retains as the comprehensible essence, the quidditas of the real experience. *Finnegans Wake* is that great epiphany of the cosmic structure resolved into language.

The Hysperic Poetic

In addition to the play of vicissitudes and recognitions that we have unearthed in the search for cultural motivations and the individuating poetics of Joyce, we find another surprise which casts an ambiguous and contradictory light upon all that we have discovered. We begin by asking what moves the author when he withdraws from the world of things into a universe of words in order to reconstruct the form of the world. The most striking key in *Finnegans Wake* is found in the description of the letter which constitutes both a definition of the book and the universe. In fact, this page of the *Wake* functions not only at three levels—as letter, as the book itself, as world—but it also serves as an erudite-archeological reference and constitutes a detailed and parodic analysis of the *Book of Kells*.[10] The phrases from the *Wake* which we have already quoted refer to that page of the medieval manuscript which begins with the word "Tunc" and thereby establishes a clear parallel between this medieval text and the Joycean work. The *Book of Kells* is one of the most superb examples of medieval Irish art, and even today it impresses us with its distorted and wild fantasy, its labyrinthine taste for abstraction, and its paradoxical invention. The qualities of these manuscripts (*The Book of Darrow*, the *Antiphonary of Bangor*, etc.) are the first manifestations of that Irish genius that extends itself to the limits of reason, always on the border of provocation and fragmentation. This tradition has given to our culture the first troubling voice of medieval Neo-Platonism, Scotus Erigena; a pitiless social critic and an inventor of "parallel" worlds, Swift; the first idealistic attack against the general notion of material reality, Berkeley; the adversary of every acquired social norm, Shaw; that polite and dreadful destroyer of bourgeois morality, Wilde; and, finally, Joyce, the anarchist of language and the greatest orchestrator of contemporary discord.

These manuscripts were born in a Christian, cultured Ireland that was defending itself against the paganism that had reconquered England, against the revival of barbarity that was depressing Gaul, and against the process of disintegration suffered by the entire Western culture. The period between the death of Boetius (already a testimony of a world in decline) and the Carolingian Renaissance was a time of suffering. It was this Ireland of visionary monks, of adventurous and bizarre saints, that was responsible for the recirculation of culture and art. It would be difficult to estimate how much western civilization owes to these obscure works of preservation. What we do know is that the works take the form of an erudite and whimsical composition, crazy and lucid, civilized and barbaric, as a continuous exercise in the decomposition and rearrangement of spoken language and figurative forms. These poets and illuminators cunningly wrought, in the silence of exile, the expressive emblem of their race.[11]

In a total refusal of realism, there was a flowering of *entrelacs*, of highly stylized and elegant animal forms in which small, monkey-like figures appear among an incredible geometrical foliage capable of enveloping whole pages. These are not repetitions like the themes of an ornamental carpet, for every line, each corymb represents an invention, a complexity of abstract, wandering spiral forms which deliberately ignore geometrical regularity. Delicate colors fan outward from red to yellow orange, from lemon to mauve. We find quadrupeds and birds, lions with bodies of other beasts, greyhounds with swans' beaks, unthinkable humanoid figures, contorted like the circus athlete who puts his head between his knees, thereby composing the initial of a letter. Beings as malleable and foldable as colored elastic are introduced into the maze of lacing; they peek out from behind abstract decorations, twist around the capital letters, and insinuate themselves between the lines. The page no longer stops before the gaze but assumes its own life. The reader no longer succeeds in choosing a reference point. There are no boundaries between animals, spirals, and *entrelacs*; everything mixes with everything. Nonetheless, figures or hints of figures emerge from the background, and the page tells a story, an inconceivable, unreal, abstract and, above all, fable-like story composed of protean characters whose identities are continuously disappearing.

This medieval *meandertale* is the model of the labyrinth upon which Joyce constructed his book. Joyce adopted this form because the Middle Ages were still, and always would be, his vocation and destiny. The *Wake* swarms with references to the Church Fathers and the scholastics. The chapter of Anna Livia is based upon the model of a medieval mystery. As for the *Book of Kells*, Joyce repeatedly said that he always took a reproduction of it wherever he went and that he had studied its techniques for hours on end in order to find inspiration for *Ulysses*.[12]

While the Irish illuminators threw themselves into the adventure of their *entrelacs*, the poets of the hysperic tradition cultivated the "African style," a form of baroque, late Latin poetics, and committed themselves to an operation that clearly anticipated that of Joyce—the invention of new words. It was the epoch in which poets forged terms like *collamen, congelamen, sonoreus, glaudifluus, glaucicomus, frangorico*. It was the epoch in which ten new ways to designate fire were invented, one of which was *siluleus*, "eo quod de silice siliat, unde et silex non recte dicitur, nisi ex qua scintilla silit." It was the epoch in which the taste for debate on purely verbal themes reached paroxysm, and it was possible, as Virgil the Grammarian relates, that the rhetoricians Gubundus and Terentius remained without eating and sleeping for fifteen days in order to debate the vocative of "ego" (finally resorting to violence). It was the epoch in which the Englishman Adhelm of Malmesbury succeeded in writing a letter in which, for a vast stretch, all the words began with the letter *P* (Primitus pantorum procerum poematorum pio potissimum paternoque praesertim privilegio panegiricum poemataque passim prosatori sub polo promulgatus. . .). It was the epoch in which we find, in that esoteric text *Hisperica Famina*, onomatopoeic descriptions which render the sounds of waves and which Joyce would have been overjoyed to have written:

> Hoc spumans mundanas obvallat Pelagus oras,
> terrestres anniosis fluctibus cudit margines.
> Saxeas undosis molibus irruit avionias
> Infima bomboso vertice miscet glareas
> asprifero spergit spumas sulco,
> sonoreis frequenter quatitur flabris. . . .[13]

It was also the time when Latin words were deliberately mixed with Greek and Hebrew terms, the time when the grammarian Virgil proposed as a science the "leporia," the art of original images (beautiful because "precieux") in which hermetic taste dictates that a poem is pleasing only if it constitutes a problem.[14] As in the period of Ausonius and along the entire descending curve of the late Roman culture, there appeared acrostics, alphabetic successions, *kenningar*, poems as calligrams, *centos*. These were none other than attempts to wring the last bit of residual beauty from an exhausted classical culture by a labor of recombination.

These were the Middle Ages to which *Finnegans Wake* is connected, the Middle Ages of crisis, withdrawal, aesthetic chicanery, and intellectual divertissement. But these were also the Middle Ages of preservation and maturity, in which the Latin language tested its erudite possibilities and refined and offered itself as a clean, sharp, essential tool for the great philosophical season of scholasticism. It was from these Middle Ages that Joyce developed the taste for etymology, perhaps from Isidorus of Seville, even before Vico. Here Joyce learned that once one verifies a causal resemblance between two words, the resemblance becomes a profound necessity which finds an essential kinship not only between the terms but between the two realities. Joyce adopted this suggestion and based his own calenbours on this technique, thus making a music of ideas from a music of sounds.[15]

Other techniques and sensibilities in Joyce's work are also of a medieval nature. The value of the interpretive labor reflects a medieval taste, the idea of aesthetic pleasure, not as the flashing exercise of an intuitive faculty but as a process of intelligence that deciphers and reasons, enraptured by the difficulty of communication. This is the pivotal element of the medieval aesthetic, indispensable for understanding works like *Le Roman de la Rose* and even *La Divina Commedia*.[16] The technique of concealing the figure of HCE under 216 different verbal disguises is also medieval, as is the mnemonic technique (also in Bruno) of treating the work as the exercise of a continuously active memory.[17]

Above all, the cultural syncretism is medieval, the propensity to accept all existing knowledge and to exhibit it as its own encyclopedia, more with a fabulous taste for the collection than a preoccupation with critical verification. The *Wake* displays before the reader the entire treasure of human culture without overdue respect for the actual limits of each system, and it utilizes any assertion as a demonstration of the eternal truth (although the Joycean truth is no longer the one to whose demonstration monks and devoted schoolmen adapted the entire repertoire of classical culture).

To conclude, a medieval rhythm runs unobserved under the entire discourse of the book and emerges clearly when one hears the text recorded directly by Joyce. There is a sort of "cantata," a uniform rhythm, the diabolic reintroduction of a type of *proportio* in the very core of disorder, like a coloring of white sound that serves as the threshold that separates pure noise from musical discourse. Its metrical unity consists of a ternary beat, a dactyl or an anapest, upon which the major variations play.[18] Thus, in the very moment that we are acclaiming him "the poet of a new phase of the human consciousness," Joyce frustrates all of our reductive efforts and reveals himself for what he is, or wanted to be and knew himself to be: the last of the medieval monks, protected by his own silence to illuminate illegible, fantastic words, not knowing if for himself or the men of tomorrow.[19]

The Poem of Transition

The search for a Joycean poetics has thus brought us to the discovery of various contrasting yet complementary poetics. *Finnegans Wake* finds a justification when seen as a playing ground of those poetics and read as a meta-linguistic discourse about itself. Except for lyrical moments of transparency, as in the episode of Anna Livia and in the final section, one might agree with Harry Levin that since the author cannot assume that anyone will know how to translate his ultraviolet allusions, the reader is consequently freed from this responsibility and can set about tasting the pleasures that the work offers him, the fragments that are comprehensible according to personal congeniality. In short, the reader finds his own individual game within the framework of the Big Game.

But even read with the appropriate key, does the work really say something? Does the reduction of the world to language have meaning for contemporary man? Or does the book remain as the instance of a delayed Middle Ages, the unfeasible reproposing of the *hysperic* aesthetics, an experiment at the mere level of the *nomina*? Were *Finnegans Wake* an extension of the Middle Ages, then Joyce's refusal of his own medievalism in the first part of the book would be an illusion. Were this the case, he would have denied the scholastic philosophy of his earlier works only to take a step backwards into the medievalism of pre-Carolingian rhetoric. Thus, it might appear that he had abandoned the scholasticism of *Ulysses*, not by that Renaissance which established a new human measure with Erasmus and Montaigne, but by a Renaissance of excess, an experimental, fantastic, and labyrinthine humanistic mood expressed by such works as Francesco Colonna's *Hypnerothomachia Polyphili*. Similarly, it might appear that Joyce had rediscovered a cabalistic and magical symbology of the book derived from the schemas of certain fourteenth- and fifteenth-century heraldic emblems that had reached Joyce through Bruno and others, steeped in theosophy and other esoteric influences through Yeats. With this, he would have thus rewritten the new *Pimander* for the civilization of relativity.[20]

Although Joyce's work might indeed be seen in this light, so too, one might understand those early stages of the Renaissance itself as a challenge to the prevailing dogmatic vision of the universe and a consequent rejection of rational forms of thought. The thinkers of the Renaissance sought to deny the ordered, static conception of the world by embracing the mystic Hebraic tradition, the esoteric revelations of the Egyptians, and the disclosures of a Neo-Platonic hermeticism. They were committed to rejecting the rationalistic balance of Aquinas and the lucid nominalism of the late scholastics who concerned themselves with immutable essences, objects not experimentally verifiable. In its place, they sought equally lucid and precise Galilean definitions which would address the mutable material of experimental observation.

In order to accomplish the jump between these two forms of thought, modern culture has been forced to cross the mystical forest where, among symbols and emblems, Lullo and Bruno, Pico and Ficino, the renewers of Hermes Trismegistus, the decoders of the Zohar, the alchemists struggling between experimentalism and magic wandered. While this was not the new science, it was the foreboding of the new new science.[21] This future scientific consciousness of the world was taking form by the study of mnemotecnics, the study of heraldry, and the questioning of hermetic texts. Later, with empirical research and mathematical definitions, this new science would progressively clarify a universe which was once seen only darkly through the mysteries of the heraldic emblems. At this historic moment, however, these early moderns knew by imagination, before mathematical formulation, that the universe was no longer a rigid hierarchy of immutable and definitive modules of order but something moving and changing. In such a universe, contradictions and oppositions do not constitute an evil to be reduced by abstract formulas, but they form the very core of reality.

In this sense *Finnegans Wake* is the book of an epoch of transition, a time in which science and the evolution of social relations propose a vision of the world that no longer obeys the schemas of other, more secure epochs yet lacks any formula for clarifying its own situation. The *Wake* attempts to paradoxically define the new world by assembling a chaotic and dizzy encyclopedia from the old one and filling it with explanations that once seemed mutually exclusive. Through this clash and the "Big Bang" of these oppositions, something new is born.

Finnegans Wake rebels agains the narrow-mindedness of modern methodologies which permit us to define only partial aspects of reality, thus eliminating the possibility of an ultimate and total definition. The *Wake* attempts to compensate for this with an assemblage of partial and provisional definitions that syncretically collide and combine in an enormous "world theater," a *clavis universalis* in which ideas are so arranged that the structure of the work results in a "mirror" of the cosmos.[22] Although philosophy maintains that "whereof one cannot speak, thereof one must be silent" (L. Wittgenstein, *Tractatus Logico-Philosophicus*, 7), *Finnegans Wake* makes the proud claim to bend language to express "everything." To this aim, language selects terms from the most disparate cultural heritages and makes possible their coexistence through the connective tissue of a language capable of grafting one thing to another and of tying together, by etymological violence, the most disparate references.

It would be presumptuous were Joyce claiming to give us, in a single book, the Christian tradition, Einstein, the occultists, Shakespeare, the history of mankind, Levy-Bruhl, Aquinas, Vico, Bruno and Cusanus, Freud and Krafft-Ebing, Aulus Gellius and Buddha, Paracelsus and Whitehead, Relativity and Kabbala, theosophy and Scandinavian epic, the mysteries of Isis and Space-Time – in order to show that, according to the Hermetic principle, *quod est inferius est superius* and that the material of Reality is supported by a mystical unity that only *Le Livre* can disclose. Were Joyce's work to imply this, then it would be a bad copy of the medieval encyclopedia or a product of the nineteenth-century occultist traditions, a curious fruit born from the tree of Madame Blavatsky.

But the proposal that Joyce makes is quite different. Not only the explicit declarations, but the letters, the interviews, the very tone of the work reveal an irony and distance in Joyce's handling of the cultural artifacts. The impressive aridity of his construction is evident: Joyce accumulates materials whose form captivates him but whose substance does not elicit his belief. It is as if Joyce offers us the entire wisdom of mankind, without determining whether or not it reflects a unique Eternal truth. He is concerned only with the cultural repertoire assembled by the whole of History.

Theoretically, one could reach into this treasury of ideas, enjoying them with the complacency of the decadent who is resigned to celebrate the deeds of an exhausted empire but is unable to confer an order upon this legacy. For Joyce, however, there exists only one possibility: to engage the whole of this wisdom and to impose upon it a new Order, that of Language. Joyce engages a reality composed of all that has been said of it and organizes this world according to rules which are derived, not from the things themselves, but from words that express things. He proposes a form of the world in language, a hypothesis offered from within the linguistic format. The world as such is not Joyce's concern.

In *Finnegans Wake* Joyce establishes the possibility of defining our universe in the "transcendental" form of language. He provides a laboratory in which to formulate a model of reality and, in so doing, withdraws from *things* to *language*. To understand the nature of reality itself, rather than the cultural models of reality, is a task that belongs neither to science nor literature but to metaphysics, and the crisis of metaphysics arises from its inadequacy to this task.

The question is whether this repertoire of n-dimensional definitions is valid for us, for no one, for the author, for the eye of God, for the dream of a fool, or for the readers of tomorrow – for the readers of a possible society in which exercise in the multiplication of signs will not appear as a game for the elite but as the natural, constructive exercise of an agile and renewed perception.

Conclusion

Once again, the main lesson that we can draw from the Joycean experience is a lesson in poetics, an implicit definition of the situation of contemporary art. From the first work to the last, we find in the opus of Joyce a dialectic that belongs not only to his personal intellectual life but to the entire evolution of our culture.

Ulysses is the image of a possible form of our world. But between the image and the real world from which it grew an umbilical cord still remains. *Ulysses'* statements about the form of the world are embodied in the representation of human behavior. The reader grasps a general discourse on things through a descent into the heart of things. *Ulysses*, a treatise on metaphysics, is also a handbook of anthropology and psychology, the *Baedeker* of the city in which each man can recognize his country. In contrast, *Finnegans Wake* defines our universe, offering us "the propositional function" to be filled with all possible contents, but it no longer provides an instrument for grasping the world. With Joyce, we recognize that the development of modern art is now tied to a sort of indeterminacy principle: when forms achieve the maximum clarity for representing a possible structure of the world, they can no longer give us concrete instructions on how to move in order to modify the world.

While Joyce was writing his last work in silence and exile, another great figure of contemporary literature made a different choice. Bertold Brecht decided that one could no longer "speak about trees" but must engage in pedagogic and revolutionary activity. Brecht realized that his decision did not eliminate the other horn of the dilemma but forced the issue into a situation of crisis and tension from which it could not escape. He knew that the trees do, in fact, matter to us and that the day may come when humanity might once again contemplate them. But our time demands a decision and Brecht chose his own road, recounting, with the story of his choice, the story of his regret.

James Joyce represents the other horn of the dilemma. His response to those who spoke of the war and the political events that were erupting in Europe ("Don't talk to me about politics, I'm only interested in style.")[23] leaves us perplexed concerning his human character, but it represents an example of an aesthetic and austere choice without half measure, that arouses in us, if not admiration, fright. While the pedagogic action of Brecht was effective because the poet assumed a legacy of stylistic techniques from the avant garde which his political passion channeled to diverse uses, the stylistic choices of Joyce could not be bent for the purposes of immediate communication without stripping his work of its quality as a cosmic model.

Thus a principle was established that would govern the entire development of contemporary art. From Joyce onwards, there are two separate universes of discourse. The first is a communication about the facts of man and his concrete relations. Here it makes sense to speak about the "content" of a story. The second carries out, at the level of its own technical structures, a type of absolutely formal discourse. Science presents an analogous situation. On one level it establishes a practical discourse about concrete things. In this case, the technical structures of science are used to establish the relationships among real events, the "content" of the world. On the second level, science develops a pure, "imaginative," and hypothetical discourse which, like non-Euclidean geometry and logic, outlines possible worlds. The relationships between these pure discourses and the universe of real events need not be immediately demonstrated; their function will be confirmed later, in a series of unforeseen mediations. The only law that rules the "existence" of these formalized worlds is their internal coherence.

Finnegans Wake is the first and most notable literary example of this tendency of contemporary art. To say that such universes of artistic discourse need not be immediately translatable into concrete "utilization" is not to repeat the standard aesthetic dictum about the uselessness of art. *Finnegans Wake* signals the birth of a new type of human discourse. This discourse no longer makes statements about the world; rather, it becomes a mirror-like representation of the world. In such discourse "things" acquire a vicarious function in respect to the words that utter them. "Things," so to speak, are used to convey words, to support and evidence them.

At the very moment that *Finnegans Wake* establishes this possibility of discourse, it reveals its own contradictions. In the domain of language, every organization or reorganization of signifiers entails a restructuring of the semantic system. In *Finnegans Wake* the form of the relationships between *signifiers* expresses new possibilities of defining something, yet the form assumed by the *signifieds* remains as the mirror of an obsolete universe. *Finnegans Wake* realizes a revolutionary network of connections between signifiers in order to tell us what we already know — namely, that everything is everything.

Finnegans Wake does not present itself as the solution to our artistic problems and, through it, of our cognitive and practical problems. It is neither a bible nor a prophetic book. It is the work which draws together a series of otherwise irreconcilable poetics and, at the same time, excludes other possibilities of life and art. Through these divergent directions, it reveals to us that our personality is dissociated, that our possibilities are complementary, that our grasp of reality is subject to contradiction, and that our attempt to define the totality of things and to dominate them is always, in certain measure, a checkmate.

Thus, *Finnegans Wake* is not for us *the* choice but only one possible choice. It is not the victory of a Verb that has succeeded in forever defining its own universe. As Joyce says, "condemned fool, anarch, egoarch, hiresiarch, you have reared your disunited kingdom on the vacuum of your own most intensely doubtful soul" (*FW* 188). If *Finnegans Wake* is a sacred book, it tells us that *in principium erat Chaos*. To make this statement, however, *Finnegans Wake* encloses Chaos within the framework of an apparent Order and thereby places us in the same situation as the apostate Stephen who uses the words of Thomas Aquinas in order to refuse family, country, and church.

The only faith that the aesthetics and metaphysics of the Chaosmos leaves us is the faith in Contradiction.

NOTES

[1] For the various drafts and the "progress" of the opus, cf. Litz (1961), Higginson (1960), Connolly (1961), Hayman (1963), Hart (1962), Budgen (1948) and Ellmann (1959), Boldereff (1959), Robinson (1959).

[2] Joyce meets Bruno very early: see the conversation with Father Ghezzi both in *SH* and in *P*. Cf. Stanislaus Joyce (1958, pp. 151-53). Cf. in *CW* (pp. 132-34), a review of *Giordano Bruno* by J. Lewis McIntyre, where Joyce stresses the possibility of arriving at the unity through the opposition of contraries and, with slight variation, quotes Coleridge: "'Every power in nature or in spirit must evolve an opposite as the sole condition and means of its manifestation; and every opposition is, therefore, a tendency to reunion'" (Essay XIII, 'The Friend'). The same review also contains an important statement: "More than Bacon or Descartes [Bruno] must . . . be considered the father of what is called modern philosophy" (*CW* 133). In a letter to Harriet Shaw Weaver (January 27, 1925 — *Letters I* 226) Joyce remarks: "His philosophy is a kind of dualism — every power in nature must evolve an opposite in order to realise itself and opposition brings reunion etc etc." Explicit quotations of Nichola da Cusa are in *FW* 63 and 163. Bruno is mentioned in *FW* more than one hundred times (e.g., "*Trionfante di bestia!*" [p. 305], an allusion to Bruno's *Lo spaccio della bestia trionfante*).

[3] "Hinc omnia in omnibus esse constat et quodlibet in quolibet. . . . In qualibet enim creature universum est ipsa creature, et ita quodlibet recipit omnia, ut in ipsum sint ipsum contractae. Cum quodlibet non possit esse actu omnia, cum sit contractum, contrahit omnia, ut sint ipsum" (*De docta ignorantia*, II, 5); even though omnia igitur ab invicem differre necesse est . . . ut nullum cum alio coincidat" (ibid., III, 1). On Cusanus cf. G. Santinello, *Il pensiero di Niccolò Cusano nella sua prospettiva estetica* (Padova: Liviana, 1958).

[4] As for this aspect of Bruno's philosophy, cf. Ernst Cassirer, *Das Erkenntnisproblem in der Philosophie und Wissenschaft der neueren Zeit* (Berlin: Bruno Cassirer, 1906), Vols. 1, 2.

[5] He read it in J. Toland's translation (*A Collection of Several Pieces with an Account of Jordano Bruno's "Of the Infinite Universe and Innumerable Worlds"* [London, 1726]). Joyce refers to Toland at two points in *FW* (cf. Atherton, 1960, p. 286).

[6] As for the relationship Bruno-Copernicus, cf. Emile Namer, "La nature chez Bruno," in *Atti del XII Congresso Internazionale di Filosofia* (Firenze: Sansoni, 1961), pp. 345 ff. Atherton (pp. 52-53) lists a series of "main axioms" of the *Wake* which are explicitly rooted in Bruno's and Cusanus' philosophy: there are an infinite number of worlds; as each atom has its own individual life (according to Bruno) so each letter in *FW* has its own individuality; each word tends to reflect in its own structure the structure of the *Wake*; each word has a predestined ambiguity (Freud) and a natural tendency to slide into another (Bruno); characters, like words, not only transmigrate from era to era (Vico and Bruno) but also tend to exchange their identities; this is most marked when they are opposite (Nichola da Cusa), etc.

[7] Hans Reichenbach, *The Direction of Time* (Univ. of California Press, 1956), II, 5. Cf. also *Philosophie der Raum-Zeit-Lehre* (Berlin and Leipzig, 1928), p. 167. Reichenbach, in *The Rise of Scientific Philosophy* (Univ. of California Press, 1951), II, 9, says that, even though the abstract structures discovered by science cannot be represented by imagination, it is possible that future generations will enjoy the capability of thinking and representing in some concrete way new spatial and temporal structures. My *Opera aperta-Forma e indeterminazione nelle poetiche contemporanee* (Milano: Bompiani, 1962) deals with the attempts of contemporary arts to give a sensible shape to the concepts of new science.

[8] Cf. for instance Bishop (1948). Tindall (1950, p. 59) speaks of Earwicker as a tetra-dimensional reality (the characters of traditional narrative are bidimensional and Bloom

is tridimensional).

⁹ Cf. Leopold Infeld on the structure of universe in *Albert Einstein: Philosopher-Scientist*, ed. P.A. Schilpp (Evanston, 1949). For a parallel between Joyce and Einstein, also see Troy (1939).

¹⁰ Cf. Robinson-Campbell, 1944, p. 90 and Atherton, 1960, part II, Chapter I. Joyce speaks of the *Book of Kells* in a letter to Harriet Shaw Weaver, 6 February 1923.

¹¹ Joyce has devoted the 1907 lecture "Ireland, Isle of Saints and Sages" to early Irish civilization (*CW* 153-74). This lecture is full of pitiful confusions which have confused even its critics. Ellmann (*CW* 160, *n*2) remarks that Joyce here mistakes Dionysius, the pseudo-Areopagite with San Denis, the patron saint of France (and the objection is correct). He then says that Joyce mistakes the pseudo-Areopagite with Dionysius Areopagite, that is, Dionysius of Athens. Joyce, however, correctly identifies pseudo-Areopagite, confused by the medievals with Dionysius of Athens but usually indicated after the Renaissance as "pseudo-Areopagite." What Ellmann does not note is that, in the same pages, Joyce twice mistakes Scotus Erigena for Duns Scotus (who lived four centuries later and who, by the way, was not an Irishman!).

¹² See Ellmann (1959, p. 559). Cf. also the letter to Harriet Shaw Weaver, January 13, 1925. As for the Holy Fathers and other medieval authors quoted in *FW*, see the impressive list given by Atherton: Augustine, Avicenna, Minucius Felix, Jerome, Ireneus.

¹³ Written about the seventh century, *Hisperica Famina* (see the F.J.H. Jenkinson edition [Cambridge, 1908]) is "a bantling no nation is anxious to claim. But the sources of the astonishing jargon would be an amusing if unprofitable quest" (H. Waddell, *The Wandering Scholars* [London: Constable, 1927], Chapter II, p. 41, *n*4). For an explicit parallel with Joyce see "The Irish Flavour of *Hisperica Famina*," in *Ehrengabe K. Strecker*, E.K. Rand (Dresden, 1931).

¹⁴ "Leporia est ars quaedam locuplex atque amoenitatem mordacitatemque in sua facie praeferens, mendacitatem tamen in sua internitate non devitans; non enim formidat maiorum metas excedere sed nulla reprehensione confunditur" (*Virgili Maronis gramatici opera*, Huemer, ed. [Leipzig, 1886]). Boldereff (1959, p. 15) deals briefly with the relationship between Virgil, Irish poetry, and Joyce.

¹⁵ Etienne Gilson (*Les idées et les lettres* [Paris: Vrin, 1932], p. 166) says that for a medieval thinker, when two words are similar, the things they designate must also be similar. This is the procedure followed by Isidorus of Seville in his etymologies, which are impressively similar in structure to Joyce's puns. To see in the word "Cadaver" a contraction of "caro data vermibus" implies a notion of language as direct embodiment of ontological truth. Cf. also Noon (1957, pp. 144-45) and McLuhan (1953).

¹⁶ Cf. Umberto Eco, "Sviluppo dell'estetica medievale," VI, 3, in *Momenti e problemi di storia dell'estetica*, I, Eco et al. (Milano: Marzorati, 1959). The medieval taste for a difficult interpretation is typical of an ideal reader suffering from an ideal insomnia.

¹⁷ Joyce loves Bruno because he was "so fantastical and middle-aged" (*CW* 133).

¹⁸ Cf. Troy (1939). Boldereff (1959, pp. 19-21) traces out in *FW* examples of all the major characters in the rhetorical style as practiced by medieval Irish poetry.

¹⁹ Edmund Wilson (1931, p. 187) was among the first to remark that "the style he has invented for his purpose works on the principle of a palimpsest: one meaning, one set of images, is written over another."

²⁰ On Joyce and occultism see Tindall (1950) and Boldereff (1959, pp. 74ff.).

²¹ Cf. Eugenio Garin, *La cultura filosofica del Rinascimento* (Firenze: Sansoni, 1961). About the magic and kabbalistic symbology of the book, cf. Garin, "Alcune osserva-

zioni sul Libro come simbolo" in *Umanesimo e simbolismo — Atti del IV Convegno Internazionale di Studi Umanistici* (Padova: Cedam, 1958).

[22] Cf. Paolo Rossi, *Clavis Universalis* (Napoli: Ricciardi, 1960).

[23] Quoted by R. Ellmann in the introduction to Stanislaus Joyce (1958, p. 23).

References to Joycean Literature in this Work

Works by James Joyce

CW   Joyce, James. *The Critical Writings of James Joyce*, ed. Ellsworth Mason and Richard Ellmann. New York: Viking Press, 1959.

FW   Joyce, James. *Finnegans Wake*. New York: Viking Press, 1939; London: Faber and Faber, 1939.

L   Joyce, James. *Letters of James Joyce*, Vol. I, ed. Stuart Gilbert. New York: Viking Press, 1957; reissued with corrections, 1966. Vols II and III, ed. Richard Ellmann. New York: Viking Press, 1966.

P   Joyce, James. *A Portrait of the Artist as a Young Man*. The definitive text corrected from Dublin Holograph by Chester G. Anderson and edited by Richard Ellmann. New York: Viking Press, 1964.

SH   Joyce, James. *Stephen Hero*, ed. John J. Slocum and Herbert Cahoon. New York: New Directions, 1944, 1963.

U   Joyce, James. *Ulysses*. New York: Random House, 1934 ed., reset and corrected 1961.

Works by Others

Atherton, James S.
1960   *The Books at the Wake: A Study of Literary Allusions in James Joyce's "Finnegans Wake"* (London: Faber & Faber, 1959; rpt. New York: Viking, 1960).

Beach, Joseph W.
1932   *The Twentieth Century Novel: Studies in Technique* (New York: Appleton-Century, 1932).

Beckett, Samuel et al.
1929   *Our Exagmination Round His Factification for Incamination of "Work in Progress"* (Paris: Shakespeare & Co., 1929).

Benco, Silvio
1922   "L'*Ulisse* di James Joyce," *La Nazione*, 5, no. 78 (April 2, 1922).

Bishop, John P.
1948   "*Finnegans Wake*," in the *Collected Essays*, ed., Edmund Wilson (London, New York: Scribner's, 1948).

Blackmur, Richard P.
1948   "The Jew in Search of a Son," *Virginia Quarterly Review*, 24 (Winter 1948).

Bolinger, Dwight L.
1950   "Rhyme, Assonance and Morpheme Analysis," *Word* (August 1950).

Broch, Hermann
1936   "James Joyce und die Gegenwart," in *Dichten und Erkennen*, vol. 6 (Zürich: Rhein Verlag, 1955).

Boldereff, Frances M.
1959   *Reading "Finnegans Wake"* (London: Constable, 1959).

Budgen, Frank
1934   *James Joyce and the Making of "Ulysses"* (London: Grayson, 1934).
1948   "James Joyce," *Horizon*, 3 (1941); rpt. in *James Joyce: Two Decades of Criticism*, ed., Seon Givens (New York: Vanguard, 1948).
1956   "Further Recollections of James Joyce," *Partisan Review*, 23 (Fall 1956).

Cambon, Glauco
1953   "Annotazioni in margine a *Ulysses*," *Aut Aut*, 16 (1953); and "Ancora su Joyce," *Aut Aut*, 17 (1953). Both essays now in *Lotta con Proteo* (Milano: Bompiani, 1963).

Connolly, Thomas E.
1961   *Scribbledehobble, the Ur-Workbook for "Finnegans Wake"* (Evanston: Northwestern Univ. Press, 1961).
1962   *Joyce's Portrait: Criticisms and Critiques* (New York: Appleton-Century-Crofts, 1962; rpt. London: Owen, 1964).

Curtius, Ernst R.
1929   "James Joyce und sein *Ulysses*," *Neue Schweizer Rundschau*, 22 (1929).

De Angelis, Giulio
1961   *"Ulysses." Guida alla lettura dell'"Ulisse"* di James Joyce (Milano: Lerici, 1961).

Dujardin, Edouard
1931   *Le Monologue intérieur: son apparition, ses origines, sa place dans l'oeuvre de James Joyce* (Paris: Messein, 1931).

Eastman, Max
1931   "Poets Talking to Themselves," *Harper's Magazine*, no. 977 (October 1931).

Eco, Umberto
1957   "Poetica ed estetica in James Joyce," *Rivista di Estetica*, no. 1 (January-April 1957).
1960   "Guida bibliografica," appendix to the Italian translation of Tindall, 1950.
1962   "Le moyen âge de James Joyce," *Tel Quel*, 11 (Autumn 1962).
1968   "Joyce et D'Annunzio: Les sources de la notion d'Epiphanie," trans. Elizabeth Hollier, *L'Arc*, 36 (1968).

Edel, Leon
1955   *The Psychological Novel, 1900-1950* (New York: Lippincott, 1955).

Eliot, T.S.
1923   "*Ulysses*, Order and Myth," *Dial*, 75 (November 1923).

Ellmann, Richard
1956   "A Portrait of the Artist as Friend," *Kenyon Reivew*, 18 (Winter 1956).
1959   *James Joyce* (New York: Oxford Univ. Press, 1959).

Empson, William
1956   "The Theme of *Ulysses*," *Kenyon Review*, 18 (Winter 1956).

Frank, Joseph
1945   "Spatial Form in Modern Literature," *Sewanee Review*, 53 (Apri 1945); rpt. in *The Widening Gyre* (Rutgers Univ. Press, 1963).

Gilbert, Stuart
1930   *James Joyce's "Ulysses"* (London: Faber & Faber, 1930).

Goldberg, Samuel L.
1961   *The Classical Temper: A Study of James Joyce's "Uysses"* (London: Chatto & Windus, 1961).

Gorman, Herbert
1940   *James Joyce* (New York: Rinehart, 1940).

Guidi, Augusto
1954   *Il primo Joyce* (Rome: Edizioni di "Storia e Letteratura," 1954).

Hart, Clive
1962   *Structure and Motif in "Finnegans Wake"* (London: Faber & Faber, 1962).

Hayman, David
1956   *Joyce et Mallarmé*, 2 vols. (Paris: Lettres Modernes, 1956).

Hayman, David, ed.
1963   *A First Draft Version of "Finnegans Wake"* (London: Faber & Faber, 1963).

Higginson, Fred H.
1960   *Anna Livia Plurabelle: The Making of a Chapter* (Minneapolis: Univ. of Minnesota Press, 1960).

Joyce, Stanislaus
1958   *My Brother's Keeper* (London: Faber & Faber, 1958).

Jung, Carl Gustav
1932   "*Ulysses*: Ein Monolog," *Europäische Revue*, 8 (September 1932).

Kaye, Julian B.
1959   "A Portrait of the Artist as Blephen-Stoom," in Magalaner.

Larbaud, Valery
1922   "James Joyce," *Nouvelle revue française*, 18 (April 1922).
1925   "A propos de James Joyce et de *Ulysse*," *Nouvelle revue française*, 24 (January 1925).

Levin, Harry
1941   *James Joyce: A Critical Introduction* (Norfolk: New Directions, 1941).

Litz, Walton
1961   *The Art of James Joyce: Method and Design in "Ulysses" and "Finnegans Wake"* (London: Oxford Univ. Press, 1961).

Magalaner, Marvin, ed.
1959   *A James Joyce Miscellany*, Second Series (Carbondale: Southern Illinois Univ. Press, 1959).

McLuhan, Marshall
1951   "Joyce, Aquinas, and the Poetic Process," *Renascence*, 4 (Autumn 1951).
1953   "James Joyce: Trivial and Quadrivial," *Thought*, 28 (1953).

Meyerhoff, Hans
1955   *Time in Literature* (Berkeley: Univ. of California Press, 1955).

Miller, Henry
1938   "The Universe of Death," *Phoenix*, 1, no. 1 (Spring 1938); rpt. in *The Cosmological Eye* (Norfolk: New Directions, 1939).

Noon, William T.
1957   *Joyce and Aquinas* (New Haven: Yale Univ. Press, 1957).

Paci, Enzo
1953   "Esistenzialismo e letteratura," in *L'esistenzialismo* (Torino: E.R.I., 1953).

Paris, Jean
1957   *James Joyce par lui-même* (Paris: Éditions de Seuil, 1957).

Pastore, Annibale
1947   "L'interpretazione filosofica della vita nell'*Ulisse* di James Joyce," *L'indagine: quaderni di critica e filosofia* (Rome), no. 1 (1947).

Pound, Ezra
1922   "Ulysses," *Dial*, 72 (1922).

Powell, Jones William
1955   *James Joyce and the Common Reader* (Norman: Univ. of Oklahoma Press, 1955).

Campbell, Joseph and Robinson, Henry Morton
1944   *A Skeleton Key to "Finnegans Wake"* (London: Faber & Faber; New York: Harcourt, Brace, 1944).

Robinson, Henry Morton
1959   "Hardest Crux Ever," in Magalaner.

Schorer, Max
1948   "Technique as Discovery," *Hudson Review*, 1 (Spring 1948).

Slocum, John J. and Cahoon, Herbert
1953   *A Bibliography of James Joyce (1882-1941)* (New Haven: Yale Univ. Press, 1953).

Spencer, Theodore
1944   "Introduction and Editorial Note," in Joyce's *Stephen Hero* (Norfolk: New Directions, 1944).

Svevo, Italo
1938   "James Joyce," *Il Convegno*, 18 (January 1938).

Tindall, William Y.
1950   *James Joyce: His Way of Interpreting the Modern World* (New York: Scribner's, 1950).
1955   *The Literary Symbol* (New York: Columbia Univ. Press, 1955).
1959   *A Reader's Guide to James Joyce* (New York: Noonday Press, 1959).

Troy, William
1939   "Notes on *Finnegans Wake*," *Partisan Review*, 6 (Summer 1939).

Wilson, Edmund
1931   "James Joyce," in *Axel's Castle: A Study in the Imaginative Literature of 1870-1930* (New York, London: Scribner's, 1931; rpt. 1959, 1969).
1947   "The Dream of H.C. Earwicker," in his *The Wound and the Bow* (New York: Oxford Univ. Press, 1947).